KU-707-950

Contents

Introduction

During the First World War, Lloyd George said that his civil servants were keeping three sets of casualty figures: one to delude the Cabinet, one to delude the public and one to delude themselves. However cynical the remark might have been, it does provide a perfect example of Britain's ambivalent relationship with statistics.

As long ago as 1538, it became obligatory in England to keep written records of all baptisms, marriages and burials. Yet as recently as 1753, a plan to take a census of the population was denounced by the Whig party as 'utterly ruining the last freedom of the English people'. Confronted with a man holding a clipboard wanting to ask us impertinent questions, we Brits have two reactions: 'How dare you invade my privacy?' and 'What have you learned about my neighbours?'

The first British census was taken in 1801, since when they've happened every ten years. It wasn't until 1841 that individual names were taken (until then the census was a simple headcount), but each subsequent questionnaire has wheedled its way further and further into our cosy domesticity. In 1871 they asked if we were an 'imbecile, idiot or lunatic'. In 1901 they enquired whether or not we worked at home. In 1911 they wanted to know – damn it – how long we'd been married. How to respond to such nosiness? Not for us the American vulgarity of Hannibal Lecter, who greeted a census taker by eating his liver with a nice Chianti. No, we Brits exact a more subtle revenge. In 2001 a campaign encouraging respondents to list their religion as 'Jedi Knight' gained 390,000 followers, putting it fourth in the list, ahead of Sikhism, Buddhism and Judaism.

And yet, and yet ... We can't help loving a good stat. Which of us can say, hand on heart, that we don't feel a little thrill when we learn that 1 in 4 British women prefer gardening to sex? Or that the UK's most dangerous sport is fishing? Or that Blackpool has more hotel beds than Portugal? Or fail to respond to the news that Britain's

8 out of 10 Brits

INTRIGUING STATISTICS ABOUT THE
WORLD'S 79TH LARGEST NATION

CHARLIE CROKER

arrow books

Published by Arrow Books 2010

2 4 6 8 10 9 7 5 3 1

Copyright © Charlie Croker 2009

Charlie Croker has asserted his right under the Copyright, Designs
and Patents Act, 1988, to be identified as the author of this work

First published in Great Britain in 2009 by
Random House Books
Random House, 20 Vauxhall Bridge Road,
London SW1V 2SA

www.rbooks.co.uk

Addresses for companies within The Random House Group Limited can be found at:
www.randomhouse.co.uk/offices.htm

The Random House Group Limited Reg. No. 954009

A CIP catalogue record for this book
is available from the British Library

ISBN 9780099532866

The Random House Group Limited supports The Forest Stewardship
Council (FSC), the leading international forest certification organisation. All our
titles that are printed on Greenpeace approved FSC certified paper carry the FSC logo.
Our paper procurement policy can be found at:
www.rbooks.co.uk/environment

Mixed Sources
Product group from well-managed
forests and other controlled sources
www.fsc.org Cert no. TT-COC-2139
© 1996 Forest Stewardship Council

Designed and Typeset by
Friederike Huber

Printed and bound in Great Britain by
CPI Bookmarque, Croydon, CR0 4TD

roads, placed end to end, would reach the moon. Should you remain unmoved by the fact that glossy magazines cause more accidents than chainsaws, you really should seek help.

A word of warning. You should use statistics as a drunk uses a lamppost – for support rather than illumination. One of the many problems is that definitions differ over time. Adam Smith, for example, excluded 'government spending and lawyers' from his measure of national wealth, as they were 'unproductive of any value'. (Doesn't that make you just love him?) And work done in the home is still excluded from GDP, leading some to comment that when a man marries his housekeeper the nation's income goes down.

But don't worry about such pedantry. Simply rejoice in the fact that while the average gym member covers 468 miles each year, the average dog walker does 676. Beam with joy on hearing that there are nearly 400 vineyards in Britain. And remember that you learn something very real about this country of ours when you know that 2,000 of its listed buildings are red phone boxes.

Charlie Croker, June 2009

The great population explosion

It's unlikely that the population of the British Isles in the Middle Ages exceeded **5** million. By 1750 it was around **10.25** million. With the arrival of the Industrial Revolution in the late 18th century the population started to climb steeply

	1800	1850	1900
England and Wales	9 million	18 million	33 million
Scotland	1.25 million	3 million	4.5 million
Ireland	5.25 million	6.5 million	4.5 million

(The Irish population was decimated by the potato famine of the mid-19th century and the mass emigration that followed.)

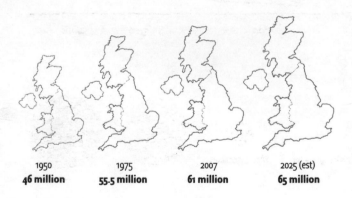

1950	1975	2007	2025 (est)
46 million	**55.5 million**	**61 million**	**65 million**

THE GROWTH OF OUR CITIES

In 1800, as the Industrial Revolution was beginning to take root, **80%** of the population lived in the countryside. By the outbreak of the First World War in 1914 **80%** of the population lived in towns

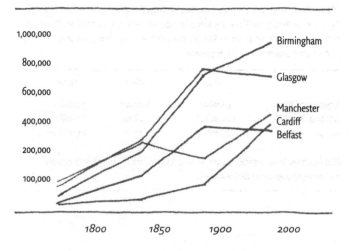

London

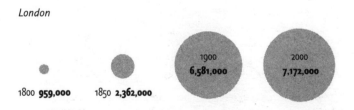

1800 **959,000**   1850 **2,362,000**

The great population explosion continues

Today, the UK is the **50th** most densely populated country in the world with 637 people per square mile (246 people per square kilometre). It comes between Guadeloupe and Jamaica. Monaco is the most densely populated country, with 32,671 people packed into its tiny area of 0.75 square miles (1.94 square kilometres). The world's least densely populated country is Greenland

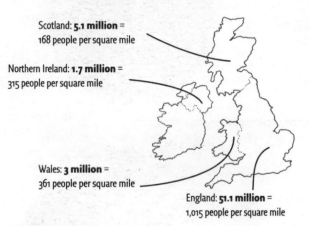

Scotland: **5.1 million** = 168 people per square mile

Northern Ireland: **1.7 million** = 315 people per square mile

Wales: **3 million** = 361 people per square mile

England: **51.1 million** = 1,015 people per square mile

Only **291** of the UK's **6,289** islands are inhabited

Around **1 in 5** people in England and Wales live in a rural area (settlements of fewer than 10,000). All of Rutland's population live in rural areas, making it the most rural county in England and Wales

Britain's smallest town is Fordwich in Kent, with a population of around **300** people

WHO'S WHO

The ethnic make-up of Britain:

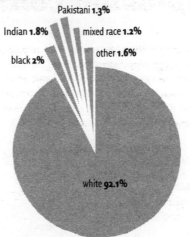

Pakistani **1.3%**

Indian **1.8%**

mixed race **1.2%**

black **2%**

other **1.6%**

white **92.1%**

The ethnic make-up of London:

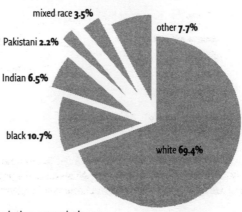

mixed race **3.5%**

other **7.7%**

Pakistani **2.2%**

Indian **6.5%**

black **10.7%**

white **69.4%**

Among the population as a whole
there are **0.98** males to every female

Births

Women of child-bearing age have, on average, just under 2 children each (**1.9**). The total fertility rate was highest in 1964, at **2.95**, and lowest in 2001, at **1.63**

Northern Ireland currently has the highest total fertility rate in Britain: **2.02**. In Scotland it is **1.73**, England is **1.92** and Wales is **1.90**

WHAT'S IN A NAME?

Top 20 names in 2008:

	Boy	Girl
1	Jack	Olivia
2	Oliver	Ruby
3	Harry	Grace
4	Charlie	Emily
5	Alfie	Jessica
6	Thomas	Sophie
7	Joshua	Chloe
8	Daniel	Lily
9	James	Mia
10	William	Lucy
11	Lewis	Amelia
12	George	Evie
13	Ryan	Ella
14	Ethan	Katie
15	Dylan	Charlotte
16	Samuel	Summer
17	Joseph	Ellie
18	Liam	Megan
19	Jake	Ava
20	Jacob	Hannah

Jack has been the most popular boy's name in England every year since 1995

In Wales, the top boy's and girl's names in 2008 were Isaac and Zoe

In Northern Ireland, Jack and Katie were the most popular boy's and girl's names in 2008

In 2008 Jack was also the most popular boy's name in Scotland, followed by Lewis, Daniel, Liam and James. For girls the top 5 were Sophie, Emily, Olivia, Chloe and Emma

In 1951 the 5 most popular names, as recorded in the births column in The Times, *were:*

	Boy	Girl
1	John	Ann(e)
2	David	Mary
3	Charles	Jane
4	Richard	Elizabeth
5	Peter	Margaret

SINGLE PARENTS, YOUNG PARENTS

Between 1971 and 2008 the proportion of lone parent households rose almost threefold to **11%**

Men are the lone parent in only **10%** of these

About **39,000** girls under 18 became pregnant in 2006; more than **7,000** of those were younger than 16

Britain's teenage pregnancy rate is now the highest in Western Europe. Every day, **21** girls under 16 become pregnant

The youngest mother recorded in recent years gave birth to a daughter in 1997, at the age of **12**

Marriages

Annual numbers of marriages rose steadily throughout the 19th and most of the first half of the 20th century. The peak came in 1972 (around **500,000** marriages across the UK); since then there has been a steady decline. The annual figure now stands at under **280,000** marriages a year (the lowest since 1895)

2% of all marriages are between people from different ethnic backgrounds

The average age at which people get married for the first time rose through the 20th century. It now stands at **31 years, 9 months and 18 days** for men and **29 years, 8 months and 12 days** for women

88% of brides take their husband's surname once married

According to a Norwich Union survey, **1 in 5** single women start saving for their wedding before there is any prospect of their getting engaged

The average engagement period is **18** months

93% of couples plan to live together, or are already doing so, before marriage

THE BIG DAY

Since 1992 civil ceremonies in England and Wales have outnumbered religious ceremonies. By 2007 there were **2** civil ceremonies for every religious ceremony

The average wedding costs **£22,858** – only just under the average annual income of £24,000

Brides pay an average of **£1,200** for their dress

 The groom's outfit costs an average of **£165**

 Being a guest at a wedding costs an average of **£300**

SAVE THE FIRST DANCE FOR ME

The top 3 songs played for the first dance at a wedding reception are:

1 *Don't Wanna Miss a Thing* (Aerosmith)
2 *Everything I Do (I Do it for You)* (Bryan Adams)
3 *Amazed* (Lonestar)

Divorces

The divorce rate in England and Wales rose sharply after the Divorce Reform Act of 1969. In the UK as a whole divorces peaked in 1993 and have levelled off since. The divorce rate in 2007 was the lowest in 30 years (**144,000** England, **13,000** Scotland, **2,900** Northern Ireland)

1 in 5 men and women in England and Wales divorcing in 2007 had had a previous marriage ending in divorce

The highest divorce rates are among men and women in their late 20s

Extramarital affairs are the commonest cause of marriage breakdown (**29%** of divorces in 2007), followed by mid-life crisis (**14%**) and family strains (**11%**)

In **93%** of the cases where a mid-life crisis causes the rift, it is the man who is having the mid-life crisis

THE GLOBAL PICTURE

Britain's divorce rate (at just over **250** divorces per 100,000 population) compares quite favourably with the 5 most maritally challenged countries

1	Russia	**530**	divorces per 100,000 population
2	Aruba	**527**	
3	USA	**419**	
4	Ukraine	**379**	
5	Belarus	**377**	

THE COST OF SEPARATION

 The biggest divorce settlement in Britain was approximately **£48 million**, paid by insurance magnate John Charman to wife Beverley in 2006 after 29 years of marriage

Other big divorce settlements include:

£30 million by Madonna to Guy Ritchie

£30 million by WPP marketing magnate Sir Martin Sorrell to former wife Sandra after 33 years of marriage

£25 million by Phil Collins to 3rd wife Orianne Cevey

£24.3 million by Paul McCartney to Heather Mills

The average length of marriage in 2005 was **11 years, 7 months and 6 days**, compared with **9 years, 10 months and 24 days** in 1996

The family

MARRIAGE VS COHABITING

Of those women aged between 55 and 59 in 2000–3, only **1 in 10** had cohabited before the age of 25. Of those women aged between 25 and 29 in 2000–3, **1 in 5** had done so

Three-quarters of women aged between 55 and 59 in 2000–3 were married by the age of 25. Among those aged between 25 and 29 in 2000–3 less than a **quarter** were married

According to the 2006 British Social Attitudes Survey, **two-thirds** of British people think there is little difference between being married and living together

However, more than half (**56%**) agree that marriage is the best kind of relationship

In the first month (December 2005) of the Civil Partnership Act, enabling same-sex couples to receive legal recognition of their partnership, almost **2,000** couples registered

The number of single-person households rose from just under **1 in 5** in 1971 to nearly **1 in 3.5** in 2008

Smaller families are becoming the norm. **6%** of families in 1971 contained 6 or more people. In 2008 that percentage had decreased by two-thirds to **2%**

Children from an Asian background are most likely to live in a family with married parents (**87%**). The figure for white children is **63%** and for black children **46%**

THE SIZE OF THE NEST

Household sizes in 1971:

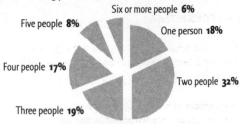

Six or more people **6%**

Five people **8%**

One person **18%**

Four people **17%**

Two people **32%**

Three people **19%**

Household sizes in 2008:

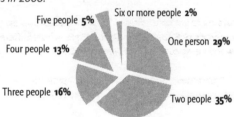

Five people **5%**

Six or more people **2%**

Four people **13%**

One person **29%**

Three people **16%**

Two people **35%**

OLDER PARENTS

In England and Wales, the average age of mothers at the birth of a first child has increased by 3 years since 1971, from **26.6** years to **29.3** years in 2007. The average age of first-time fathers has also risen, from **27.2** years in 1971 to **31.7** years in 2001 (for births registered by both parents)

LEAVING THE NEST ... OR NOT

The number of people in their 20s still living with their parents has risen significantly recently. Cost of housing is consistently given as the main reason. However, over **1 in 10** say that they 'want home comforts without the responsibility'

For whom the bell tolls

LIFE EXPECTANCY

How we compare with other nations:

Country	Rank	Life Expectancy (Yrs)
Macau	1	84.33
Japan	3	82.07
France	9	80.87
Italy	18	80.07
Greece	25	79.52
United Kingdom	**36**	**78.85**
Bosnia and Herzegovina	42	78.33
United States	45	78.14
United Arab Emirates	71	75.89
The Bahamas	162	65.72
Cambodia	176	61.69
South Africa	207	48.89
Swaziland	223 (lowest)	31.99

Life expectancy inevitably varies from area to area within each country. In the UK, the discrepancy in Glasgow is particularly marked: men in the city's Calton area have a life expectancy of **54**, whereas 5 miles away in Lenzie their counterparts can expect to live to **82**

KICKING THE BUCKET

The highest annual number of deaths in the UK in the 20th century was in 1918 (**715,200**) at the time of an influenza pandemic

From the 1950s the annual number of deaths rose slightly, reaching a peak of **675,600** in 1979, and then starting to fall. This decline is projected to level off in the early 2010s

Deaths are then expected to increase again to **800,000** deaths a year by 2051. Much of the increase will come as the 1960s 'baby boom' generation reach old age

In every year since 1901, with the exception of 1976, there have been more births than deaths

Infant mortality (under 1 year) has dropped from **30 per 1000** in 1951 to **4.8 per 1000** in 2007

LIVING LONGER

In the 2001 census, for the first time ever there were more people over 60 than under 16. At the end of the 19th century, by contrast, more than a third of those living in England were aged under 15

As of 2005, the average person in the UK spends **35 years** as a grandparent, longer than any other stage of their life

The average age of the first-time grandparent is **49**

In 2007 there were almost **3 times** as many women as men aged 90 or over as in 1971 (417,000 altogether, compared with 125,000 in 1971)

In 2007 only **4%** of deaths occurred at ages under 45

The Grim Reaper

CAUSES OF DEATH

Since the early 1970s, circulatory diseases (including heart disease and stroke) have remained the most common cause of death among males and females in the UK

However, they have also shown the greatest decline, particularly among males

Death rates for circulatory diseases, per million of population:

	Males	Females
1971	6,900	4,300
2005	2,600	1,700

Cancer is the **2nd** most common cause of death among both sexes in the UK. A third of the population will develop cancer at some point in their lives and a quarter will die of it

SUICIDE

Suicide has recently become a young man's game. Until the end of the 1980s men aged 65 and over were the most likely to kill themselves, the rate peaking at **26 per 100,000** population in 1986. By 2005 this had fallen to **17**

Suicides among men aged 25–44, however, rose from **14 per 100,000** in 1971 to a peak of **27 per 100,000** in 1998. It has since declined, but in 2005 was still the highest of all age groups, at **22 per 100,000**

Since the early 1990s the Scottish suicide rate has regularly been **50%** higher than the average for Britain as a whole. A report commissioned by the Scottish Government suggests that the high suicide rate is alcohol- and drug-related

Within England, the highest suicide rates are in the Northwest and Northeast (men) and Northwest and London (women)

The suicide rate among the homeless is **35 times** that of the general population

Men have always been more prone to suicide than women, but the gap is widening, from about **1.5** men committing suicide to every woman in 1973 to **3** men per woman in 2005

In the 4 weeks that followed Princess Diana's funeral in 1997, the overall suicide rate in England and Wales rose by **17%**, compared with the average reported for that period in the 4 previous years. The greatest increase in suicides (up by nearly a half) was among women aged 25 to 44

FINAL RESTING PLACE

Proportion of British people cremated: **72%** (average cost of cremation in 2000: £1,215)

Proportion of British people buried: **28%** (average cost of burial in 2000: £2,048)

There is now such a shortage of burial space in the UK that it is estimated that by 2020 some areas of the country will have no space at all for new interments

Where we live

A VERY DES RES?

Houses rather than flats are the British hallmark, with **82%** of families living in a house, and only **16%** in a flat. In Spain, Italy and Germany, by contrast, half the population are flat-dwellers; in France the figure is **41%**

British homes are the smallest in Europe, with an average usable floor space of **818** square feet (76 square metres). The prize for the most expansive homes goes to Italy, where the average usable floor space is **990** square feet (92 square metres)

32% of us live in detached houses. In land-rich America, by contrast, over **60%** of the population live in detached houses

RENT OR BUY?

Home ownership is prized in Britain – **69%** of us own the place we live in. This puts us towards the top of the European league table – equal with Italy though behind Spain (**80%**). Home ownership stands at **54%** in France and **43%** in Germany

Only **1 in 9** British homes are rented privately, and Britain has the highest provision of 'social housing' (council or Housing Association) in Europe (**22%**)

LIVING CHEEK BY JOWL

> Since 1900 the population of the UK has nearly **doubled**, but the number of dwellings has more than **tripled**

New households in England are being formed at the rate of **223,000** per year, with 1-person households accounting for **155,000** of these. One third of all 1-person households are aged over 65 years

> Two connected recent trends have been towards greater density of home building and an increase in the proportion of flats built. In 1991–2 over a **quarter** of new dwellings in England were flats; this fell to just under **1 in 5** towards the end of the decade, but rose to nearly **1 in 2** in 2005–6

> Between 1995 and 2005 the average density of new homes built in England increased from **24** to **40** per hectare (from 59 to 99 per acre). The increase was especially large in London, where the density doubled

HOUSEHOLD CHORES

> Women still do the majority of household chores, spending nearly **3 hours** a day on housework; men spend on average **1 hour 40 minutes**. This may explain why men on average have **30 minutes** more free time each day than women – but then women spend an average of **14 minutes** more in bed

Ironing clothes is the least popular activity among both sexes

The property ladder

HOUSE PRICES: THE ETERNAL OBSESSION

Until the early 1980s the average price of a house was well under **£20,000** (it rose from £2,049 in 1958 to £13,820 20 years later). Everything, however, changed with the 80s housing boom

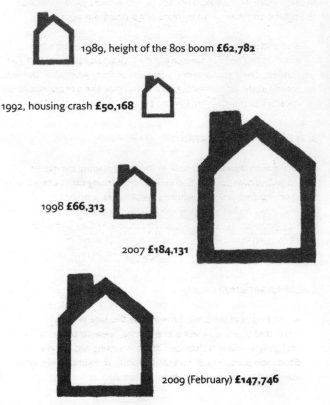

1989, height of the 80s boom **£62,782**

1992, housing crash **£50,168**

1998 **£66,313**

2007 **£184,131**

2009 (February) **£147,746**

Crashes in the 1970s and early 1990s saw up to **30%** wiped off the value of houses. By the end of 2008 the average house had lost **19%** of the value it had had a year earlier

> Between August 2007 and August 2008 UK web searches for 'houses for sale' decreased by more than **50%**

MILLIONAIRE'S ROW

In 2007 there were **88,000** houses valued at more than £1 million in England and Wales – an increase of **58,000** from 2002

> Kensington Palace Gardens is probably the most expensive street in the UK: the average value of a property there is over **£41 million**. The top 20 streets in England in 2007 were all in London, mostly in the postcodes W8 and SW3, while the 3 most expensive counties in the UK were Greater London, Surrey and Berkshire

A PLACE IN THE COUNTRY

As for the most expensive house in the UK, a leading candidate has to be Updown Court in Surrey. It offers, among other things, 5 swimming pools, a glass-walled squash court, a private cinema, a 2-lane bowling alley in the basement, several reception rooms, 13 bedrooms, 20 bathrooms and 43 lavatories, all set in 11 acres of landscaped gardens and 46 acres of woodland. It was on the market at **£70 million** in mid-2007

CHEAPER PICKINGS

> At the height of the latest housing bubble, one survey suggested that the lowest average prices were to be found in Lochgelly in Fife and Blaenau Gwent (hovering around the **£100,000** mark). South Yorkshire and South Humberside were identified as the cheapest areas in the UK

The kitchen

FIXTURES AND FITTINGS

*By 2007 the following items of kitchen equipment were thought to be
sufficiently widespread to merit inclusion in the Consumer Prices Index:*

cooker (gas cookers first appeared in the 1880s; the first electric
cooker was in 1893. Neither became common in the UK until after
the Second World War)

fridge (the first practical modern fridge appeared in 1915 and by the
1930s **60%** of US households owned one. Yet it took the UK until
the 1970s to reach a similar level of fridge ownership. By 2006 the
figure was **97%**)

freezer (freezers, as opposed to freezer compartments in fridges,
did not become widespread until the 1970s)

microwave oven (the first microwave oven was built by Radarange
in 1947. It was nearly 6 feet (1.8 metres) tall, weighed 750 pounds
(340 kilograms) and cost about $5000. **91%** of UK homes now have
a microwave)

dishwasher (the dishwasher was first unveiled in 1893, the
brainchild of Josephine Cochrane, who never washed dishes herself
but was prompted to invent the device because her servants were
chipping her fine china. **38%** of UK homes now have a dishwasher.
On average they use it 4 times per week. Dishwashers account for
8% of UK household water consumption)

washing machine (in 1948, when **52%** of American households
owned an electric washing machine, only **4%** of British households
did. By 2006 the British figure was **96%**. On average, people in the
UK use their machine 4 times per week, and washing machines
account for **15%** of UK household water consumption)

THE DECLINE OF THE GREAT BRITISH BREAKFAST

In 1976 **18%** of people ate a cooked breakfast, **40%** ate a cereal breakfast (twice as many as in the 1950s) and **25%** had bread, toast or a roll

17% had no breakfast or only a drink

By 2005, **over half** the population was no longer eating breakfast

88% of breakfasters eat the meal at home. In London **15%** eat it at work. **63%** of office workers have breakfast 5 times a week

Amongst 25–34-year-olds, nearly **1 in 5** consume breakfast either standing up or moving about. **90%** of the over-55s sit down to eat and drink their breakfast at home

Popular choices at breakfast include:

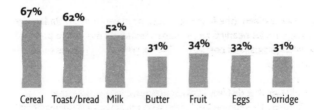

Cereal	Toast/bread	Milk	Butter	Fruit	Eggs	Porridge
67%	62%	52%	31%	34%	32%	31%

Choices of milk on breakfast cereal are as follows, according to a recent survey:

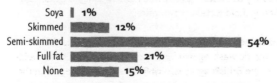

Soya	1%
Skimmed	12%
Semi-skimmed	54%
Full fat	21%
None	15%

(percentages add up to more than 100 as some people said they used more than one type of milk)

The living room

OR SHOULD THAT BE LOUNGE?

Names given to the main living area in a house:

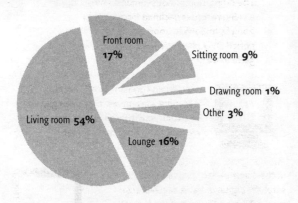

Front room **17%**

Sitting room **9%**

Drawing room **1%**

Other **3%**

Living room **54%**

Lounge **16%**

CREATURE COMFORTS

98% of British homes have fitted carpets, compared with **16%** in France and **2%** in Italy

In 1972 just over a third of households in Britain had central heating. By 2001 this had risen to **91%** for England, **92%** for Wales and **93%** for Scotland

According to a Crown Paint survey **4 in 10** of us reckon we have no flair for interior design

TAKING IT EASY

In 2005 the average British male spent
2 hours and 50 minutes each day watching
television or a DVD or listening to the radio or music.
The average for women was **25 minutes** less

The proportion of households owning
a video recorder declined from **90%** in
2003–4 to **82%** in 2006. In the same
period DVD player ownership rose from
50% to **83%**

Between 1999 and 2006, homes
owning a computer rose from **33%**
to **67%**, and those with an internet
connection from **10%** to **59%**

In the same period, households with a
satellite, digital or cable receiver rose
from **28%** to **71%** (83% if the household
contained children; 66% if not)

The bathroom

FIXTURES AND FITTINGS

The 1970s witnessed a colour explosion in bathroom furnishings, avocado proving particularly popular. Today, on the other hand, **95%** of bathroom furnishings sold in the UK are in various shades of white

KEEPING CLEAN

63% of people prefer to shower rather than take a bath

The preference is more marked among men (**72%**) than women (**53%**)

Average time taken in shower (in minutes per day):

Women ▬▬ **8.4 min**
Men ▬▬ **7.6 min**

Average time taken in the bathroom in total:

Women ▬▬▬▬▬ **27.5 min**
Men ▬▬▬▬ **20.7 min**

On a night-out:

Women ▬▬▬▬▬▬▬▬▬ **59.1 min**
Men ▬▬▬▬▬ **36.4 min**

36% of people do not take a bath or shower every day

6% bathe once a week   **1%** bathe once a month

THE MALE OF THE SPECIES

As findings on the average length of time spent in the bathroom suggest, men do not always take cleanliness to heart ...

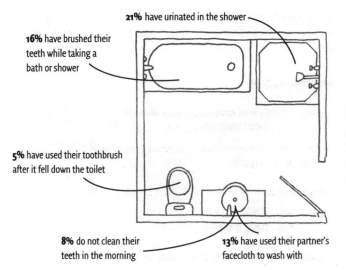

21% have urinated in the shower

16% have brushed their teeth while taking a bath or shower

5% have used their toothbrush after it fell down the toilet

8% do not clean their teeth in the morning

13% have used their partner's facecloth to wash with

12% identified their grooming habits as similar to those of Robbie Williams – the same percentage as those who said theirs were similar to Homer Simpson's

SMALL ROOM, BIG IDEAS

1 in 8 business bosses have said that they get their best ideas while relaxing in the bath. This seems to accord with the findings of another survey, which revealed that **40%** of people say that the bathroom is the only place they get time to themselves

The smallest room

QUALITY TIME

36% of people spend between 10 and 20 minutes
a day (2.5 and 5 days a year) on the toilet

    1% of people spend over 13 days a year on the loo

A 2001 survey of 159 male and 20 female Westminster MPs
found that **half** the men got up to urinate at least once a
night. **35%** of the women MPs did so

    Women are **3** times more likely to have to
queue before using the toilet than men

A 2008 survey found that in the preceding month **75%** of people had
encountered a toilet that was dirty, unflushed, or had no loo roll

    1 in 10 house-sellers admit that when leaving
the property they take the toilet roll holders
(and towel rails) with them

    11% of people do not wash their hands after going to the toilet

TOILET RECREATION

A 2008 survey found that while on the toilet:

    39% of people read

    21% of people text

    21% of people talk (on the phone or to a family member)

A separate survey found that **49%** of men read on the toilet, compared to **26%** of women. Newspapers were the most popular reading matter (**14%**) compared to magazines (**10%**), books (**8%**) and household bills (**4%**)

Women are less likely (**8%**) than men (**12%**) to chat to a family member

REGIONAL VARIATIONS

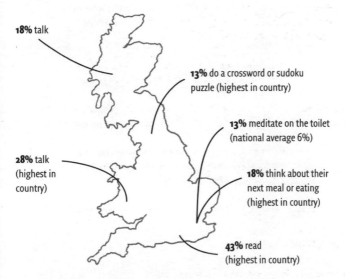

18% talk

13% do a crossword or sudoku puzzle (highest in country)

13% meditate on the toilet (national average 6%)

28% talk (highest in country)

18% think about their next meal or eating (highest in country)

43% read (highest in country)

OCCUPATIONAL HAZARDS

A 2004 survey found that **1 in 4** people have lost jewellery down the loo, while **1 in 50** have lost money (including 1 person who dropped an entire wage packet down there). Other lost items included false teeth and mobile phones. One respondent had flushed away his wedding ring while on his honeymoon

Retiring to bed

CAN I STAY UP A BIT LATER?

1 in 5 parents say that they regularly argue with their children about bedtime, while just under **1 in 10** say that they bribe their children to help with household chores by allowing them to stay up later

87% of parents believe that children nowadays go to bed later than they did as children (5-year-olds are thought to need 10 to 12 hours sleep each night; 10-year-olds need 9.5 to 11.5 hours)

7 in 10 children have a television in their bedroom, while 6 in 10 have a games console

1 in 20 parents say their child's room has more valuable items in it than any other room in the house

44% of children are sent to bed between 9pm and 12am on a school night

THE END OF A LONG DAY

40% of adults go to bed between 10 and 11pm during the week

12% of adults go to bed at 9pm during the week

40% of adults rarely or only sometimes go to bed at the same time as their partner and **1 in 4** couples always or regularly sleep apart

Before getting into bed, **22%** of people charge electrical appliances, while **10%** of people pray

While in bed, **1 in 3** people make phone calls, or send or receive texts or emails

9% of people take coffee to bed – the same proportion who take alcohol

DRESSING FOR THE OCCASION

	Men	Women
Wear pyjamas	**21%**	**37%**
Wear nothing	**40%**	**22%**
Other apparel, e.g. underwear	**39%**	**41%**

1 in 100 men claim to wear a nightie

Bedroom antics

SLEEPING TOGETHER

Sleeping positions of couples:

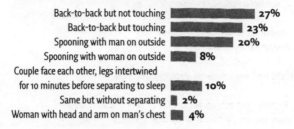

Back-to-back but not touching **27%**
Back-to-back but touching **23%**
Spooning with man on outside **20%**
Spooning with woman on outside **8%**
Couple face each other, legs intertwined
for 10 minutes before separating to sleep **10%**
Same but without separating **2%**
Woman with head and arm on man's chest **4%**

92% of couples stick to the same side of the bed each night

On average, men sleep for **8 hours and 4 minutes** and women for **8 hours and 18 minutes**

THE CURSE OF SNORING

An estimated **15 million** adults in the UK snore – 10.4 million males, 4.5 million females

Men's snoring is perceived to be louder

58% of snorers are between 50 and 59 years of age

41% of people say snoring keeps them awake – of these people, **55%** say snoring actually causes arguments

DREAMING DREAMS

96% of people have dreamed 1 or more of the following standard anxiety dreams: inability to walk or run, inability to speak or scream, teeth coming loose/falling out, flying, being naked in public, having relationships with people you don't fancy, death of friends or family and being back at school or taking exams

23% of people have had sexy dreams about someone they know

4% have had sexy dreams about celebrities

3% have had sexy dreams about 'any random person' ('faceless or just blobs of light or shape')

2% have had sexy dreams about themselves

0.5% have had sexy dreams about their boss

Of that first **23%**, the 'someone they knew' was:

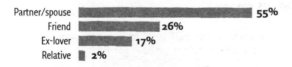

Partner/spouse	**55%**
Friend	**26%**
Ex-lover	**17%**
Relative	**2%**

HORIZONTAL JOGGING

In the course of their lifetime the average Briton will have sex **4,239** times

In 2000 **124** people were injured by sex aids. The number rose to **179** in 2001 and went up to **451** in 2002

The garage

CAR WORSHIP

Number of cars in Britain:

			25 million
		11.5 million	
	8 million		
2.25 million			
1951	1964	1970	2004

	1971	2007
Households with no cars	**48%**	**23%**
Households with 1	**45%**	**45%**
Households with 2	**6%**	**27%**
Households with 3+	**1%**	**6%**

The most popular car in 2008, for the tenth consecutive year, was the Ford Focus. Over **101,500** Focuses were sold, with the Vauxhall Corsa's sales of 99,500 coming 2nd

Sales of new cars were down from **2.4 million** in 2007 to **2.1 million** in 2008 (a decline of **11.3%**). August sales were the lowest since 1966

There are **4** motoring offences a year for every **10** vehicles

WHO'S DRIVING?

Between 1988 and 2008 the number of women drivers in the UK rose from **10.2 million** to **15.3 million**. Contrary to popular male prejudice, though, the number of people killed or seriously injured on the roads fell (according to police statistics)

Between 1997 and 2007 the proportion of people over 70 holding driving licences rose from **38%** to **52%**

From the mid-1990s to the mid-2000s, the proportion of people aged 17–20 with a driving licence fell from **48%** to **28%**. Reasons include cost and the increasing difficulty of passing the driving test – pass rates have dropped 10% since the early 1990s

The British driving test was inaugurated in 1935 and nearly **92 million** people have taken it – 1.8 million people took it in 2006–7

Average time spent preparing for test:	**14 months**
Average number of professional lessons:	**52 hours; cost £1,200**
First-time pass rate in 2006–7:	**43%**
Average number of tests before passing:	**2.3**

In **1 of 5** driving tests where the candidate failed, he or she performed so badly that the instructor had to 'physically intervene'

According to a Diamond survey, **41%** of Britons have made love in their car – **52%** of men and **34%** of women

The working week

At the beginning of the 20th century, the length of the average working week in the UK was over **50 hours**

This fell to around **35 hours** by the end of the 1970s (because of legislation, higher productivity, and also because of the rise in part-time working as more women entered the workforce)

In the 1980s, this downward trend stopped, mainly as a result of a shift towards employment in occupations where long hours prevail, such as self-employment and managerial and professional jobs

But the second half of the 1990s saw a return to the trend towards shorter working hours – for full-time workers, at least

Hours worked per week:

	Full-time workers	*Part-time workers*
1996	**38.7**	**15.1**
2000	**37.9**	**15.4**
2004	**37.3**	**15.6**
2008	**37.0**	**15.5**

Within these averages, however, lie a significant proportion of people who do a lot of work: **20.4%** of the workforce (6 million people) work over **45 hours** per week

UK workers have **20 days** paid leave per year. This compares to 25–30 in most EU countries – but is higher than Japan (17 days) and the United States (10 days)

KEEPING YOUR MIND ON THE JOB - OR NOT

63% of people admit to wasting time at work.
The average amount wasted in an 8.5-hour day is 1.7 hours

The major causes of time-wasting are,
according to those surveyed:

personal internet use **34.7%**

socialising with fellow workers **20.3%**

conducting personal business **17%**

Some so-called 'work-related' activities are in themselves
felt to be a waste of time:

correcting someone else's work **18.1%**

office politics **16.2%**

dealing with emails **13.1%**

A third of office workers have watched porn
in the office; **7%** have been caught in the act

62% have had an office romance; **28%** have
fallen asleep at their desks (presumably, this
group does not overlap with the 62% who have
had an office romance)

The jobs we do

THE WAGE PACKET

The average annual salary in 2008 was approximately **£24,000**. Among company directors and CEOs, the average was £213,000; over the past few years this group has seen a higher annual increase in salary than any other. The next highest-paid group of workers were brokers (£94,000), financial managers (£77,000), aircraft pilots and engineers (£64,000) and mining and energy managers (£59,000)

The worst-paid full-time job is probably that of library assistants. In 2008 they earned on average **£11,000** per year

Annual salaries, 2008 BBC survey:

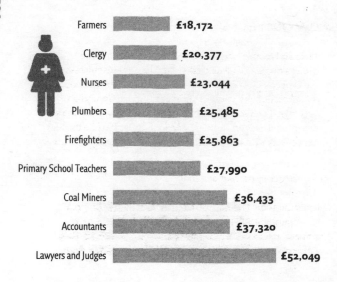

Farmers	£18,172
Clergy	£20,377
Nurses	£23,044
Plumbers	£25,485
Firefighters	£25,863
Primary School Teachers	£27,990
Coal Miners	£36,433
Accountants	£37,320
Lawyers and Judges	£52,049

The average advertised London salary (**£41,500**) is more than £10,000 higher than those advertised in the rest of the UK

DANGEROUS JOBS

Positions 2 to 7 in the list of 'most dangerous jobs performed by UK people' are occupied by the following professions: bomb disposal/mine clearance expert, oil/gas rigger, construction worker, lorry/commercial driver, deep-sea diver and war-zone security guard

Construction workers, for instance, suffer a death rate of **3.7** workers per 100,000

The most dangerous job, however, is fisherman or merchant seafarer – the death rate for fishermen is **103** per 100,000, **27 times** the level for construction workers

WILL MY JOB KILL ME?

Male and female non-manual workers – who include professionals as well as clerks – had the greatest increase in life expectancy from 1972 to 2005. The average male worker in a non-manual job saw his life expectancy go from 71.2 to 79.2 years, an increase of **8** years. A male manual worker, on the other hand, saw an increase of only **6.8** years; while the life-expectancy of a female manual worker went up by only **4.8** years

Life expectancy by occupation (2005):

Non-manual man	79.2
Manual man	75.9
Non-manual woman	82.9
Manual woman	80.0

Women vs men

THE RISE OF THE WORKING WOMAN

One of the greatest spurs to female emancipation in the 20th century workplace was the First World War. Between 1914 and 1918, 2 million women replaced men in employment. The proportion of women in total employment rose from **24%** in July 1914 to **37%** by November 1918

The sort of work women did changed, too. From the 19th century to 1911, between **11%** and **13%** of the female population in England and Wales had been domestic servants. By 1931, that figure had dropped to under **8%**

The number of women in the Civil Service, on the other hand, increased from **33,000** in 1911 to **102,000** by 1921

THE ERA OF EQUALITY?

Average hourly earnings for full-time employees (excluding overtime):

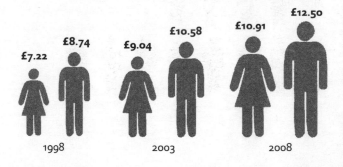

£7.22 £8.74 £9.04 £10.58 £10.91 £12.50

1998   2003   2008

This means that an average man working full-time
is paid **£27,000** a year, **£6,000** more than a woman

In 2008 **79%** of men and **70%** of women of
working age were employed. This figure has
remained unchanged for nearly 10 years

Nearly **three-quarters** of Britain's
3.8 million self-employed are men

Men are **10** times more likely than women
to be employed in skilled trades

1 in 5 women in employment do administrative
or secretarial work, compared with **1 in 25** men

Almost **half** of all working women work part-time,
as compared with a **sixth** of men

In the 2007 British Social Attitudes Survey nearly
1 in 5 women said that they worked because they
enjoyed it. Only **1 in 8** men felt the same way

Morality in the workplace

FAIR'S FAIR

Proportion of people surveyed who thought the profession in question was 'fair':

Profession	Percentage
Investment managers	4%
Politicians	4%
Estate agents	5%
Pension companies	7%
Traffic wardens	7%
Insurance companies	10%
Financial advisers	12%
Accountants	14%
Lawyers	14%
Building societies	24%
Banks	29%
Supermarkets	30%
Charities	35%
Police	36%
Teachers	42%
Doctors	64%

LYING ON YOUR CV

A 2008 analysis of job applications in the financial services industry found that women were **25%** more likely to lie on their CVs than men

Two-thirds of the CVs inspected in a 2004 survey contained inaccuracies; **55%** had employment discrepancies and **36%** changed academic details

CALLING IN SICK

According to a CBI survey,
12% of absences from work
are probably not for genuine reasons

In the public sector workers take an
average of **9** days sick leave each year.
In the private sector the figure is **5.8** days

3 out of 4 people who are unwell nevertheless
struggle to work. Those who are most likely to
go to work when ill are white-collar workers and –
for reasons that are not entirely clear – those based
in the West Midlands

In January 2008, a record 3.6 million workers –
1 in 8 staff – called in sick, due to the winter
vomiting bug norovirus. The outbreak was said
to have cost the economy £40 million per day
in lost productivity

JOB (DIS)SATISFACTION

Just over half of those surveyed by The Work
Foundation said their work was 'a means to
an end'. Over three-quarters of respondents
described themselves as 'satisfied', with only
11% dissatisfied. **9%** agreed with the statement
'I regard my work as meaningless'

Hobbies and pastimes

Top 6 leisure activities in 2006–7:

Men	Women
1 Watching television	1 Watching television
2 Spending time with friends/family	2 Spending time with friends/family
3 Listening to music	3 Shopping
4 Eating out	4 Reading
5 Sport/exercise	5 Listening to music
6 Reading	6 Eating out

THE GREAT OUTDOORS

77% of adults say that they walk for pleasure at least once a month

Slightly more men (**48%**) than women (**41%**) walk more than 2 miles (3.2 kilometres) every month, but women make more journeys on foot (278) than men (246) each year

Trainspotting maintains a fan base. Around **35,000** hardcore fans subscribe to *The Railway Magazine* each year

Angling is reckoned to be one of Britain's top passions – worth some £3 billion a year. In 2005 the Environment Agency stated that **11%** of the population had gone fishing at some point

INDOOR PURSUITS

The top leisure activity is watching sport, which in 2004-5 attracted **76%** of men and **60%** of women

Among retired people, surfing the internet came top in one survey (**41%**), followed by DIY and gardening (**39%**)

4 million women in the UK have an interest in knitting and/or sewing, of whom 1.5 million are 'very interested'. **448,000** men have an interest, of whom 143,000 are 'very interested'

In 2006 the average knitter spent **£165** on their hobby

Judging from sales of fan magazines, stamp collecting is about **half** as popular as knitting

KEEPING (MODERATELY) FIT

Top 5 physical activities (of those aged over 16 who had engaged in the activity during the previous 4 weeks):

1   Walking **35%**
2   Swimming **14%**
3   Keep fit/yoga **12%**
4   Cycling **9%**
4   Snooker/pool/billiards **9%**

In 2005 it was estimated that there were 4.5 million gym members in the UK. Only **27%** of them went to the gym on a regular basis

Glued to the box

In 1951 **42,000** homes in the UK had television sets. By 1963 this had risen to **13 million**

During this period, for each new television licence purchased, almost 80 fewer cinema tickets were sold

Today **25.9** of the 26.6 million households in Britain have a television set; **22.3 million** of them have digital TV

Proportion of a country's population owning a TV set:

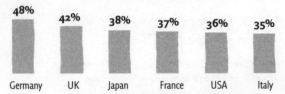

Germany	UK	Japan	France	USA	Italy
48%	42%	38%	37%	36%	35%

The number of TV sets in all these countries combined comes to only four-fifths of the total number of TV sets in China, even though only **26%** of the Chinese population own one

People in the UK watch an average of **219** minutes of television per day. This is slightly more than France (206 minutes) and Germany (211 minutes) but less than Italy (237 minutes), the USA (271 minutes) and Japan (311 minutes)

Television is now increasingly becoming an online activity.
Percentage of people watching online television:

Daily	6%
Weekly	54%
Monthly	81%

HAVE YOU SEEN?

Top 5 TV audiences:

1 1966 World Cup Final: England v West Germany **32.3 million**
2 1997 funeral of Diana, Princess of Wales **32.1 million**
3 1969 Royal family documentary **30.6 million**
4 1986 *EastEnders* Christmas episode **30.1 million**
5 1970 Apollo 13 splashdown **28.6 million**

The most popular TV programmes today are *Coronation Street* and *EastEnders*. Monday night's episodes are the most watched, with weekly viewings of around **11** and **10 million** respectively

An average of **6** films a day were shown on television in 2007, of which **25%** were British films

Viewing figures for these films totalled nearly **20** times the number of cinema admissions for the year

WHAT WE WATCH

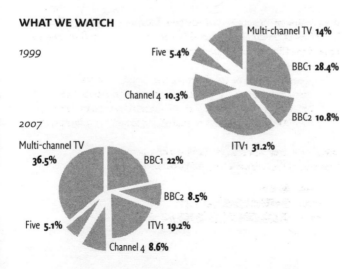

1999

Multi-channel TV **14%**
Five **5.4%**
BBC1 **28.4%**
Channel 4 **10.3%**
BBC2 **10.8%**
ITV1 **31.2%**

2007

Multi-channel TV **36.5%**
BBC1 **22%**
BBC2 **8.5%**
Five **5.1%**
ITV1 **19.2%**
Channel 4 **8.6%**

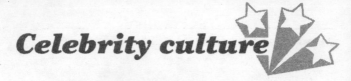

Celebrity culture

WE HATE CELEBRITIES

Viewing figures for the finale of the first series of *Big Brother* were **9.5 million** in 2000, but only just over half that in 2008

Atom bomb: voted worst idea of all time in a 2008 BBC Survey

Reality TV: voted 2nd worst idea of all time

WE LOVE CELEBRITIES

During the first 12 weeks of 2009, **24%** of Google News searches were celebrity-related. Business and finance accounted for just **10%**

The 10 biggest celebrity role models for schoolchildren in 2008, according to the Sun:

1　David Beckham (**53%**)
2　Victoria Beckham (**30%**)
3　Frank Lampard (**26%**)
4　Keira Knightley (**25%**)
5　David Tennant (**23%**)
6　Paris Hilton (**23%**)
7　Lewis Hamilton (**21%**)
8　Sugababes (**21%**)
9　Leona Lewis (**20%**)
10　Nadine Coyle from Girls Aloud (**17%**)

Top 10 'love to hate' figures in 2008, according to onepoll.com:

1   Jade Goody
2   Wayne Rooney
3   Janet Street-Porter
4   Amy Winehouse
5   Katie Price
6   Russell Brand
7   Jackiey Budden
8   Coleen McLoughlin
9   Cheryl Cole
10   Chris Eubank

THE POWER OF THE CELEBRITY ENDORSEMENT

The number of babies given the first name 'Leona' **tripled** in 2007, the year after Leona Lewis won *The X Factor*

> After Charlotte Church named her daughter 'Ruby' in 2007, it became the **2nd** most popular name for baby girls

Amy Winehouse's recent troubles are thought to have led to the name 'Amy' falling **3** places in popularity for baby girls in 2008

THE TRAPPINGS OF CELEBRITY

Wayne Rooney and Coleen McLoughlin's wedding in 2008 is estimated to have cost **£5 million**. The wedding was voted the 'most tasteful celeb wedding ever', according to onepoll.com, beating that of Prince Charles and Camilla Parker-Bowles in 2005

> *Tatler*'s best-dressed woman of 2009 was Cheryl Cole
> Meanwhile *Esquire* selected Prince Charles as their
> best-dressed man. Ronnie Corbett was 2nd

A 2009 Specsavers poll declared Elton John
to be Britain's most iconic wearer of spectacles

Computers

A NATION OF GEEKS?

In 2000 less than **half** of all households in the UK had a computer; by 2007 **70%** had one

Average number of minutes per week spent online:

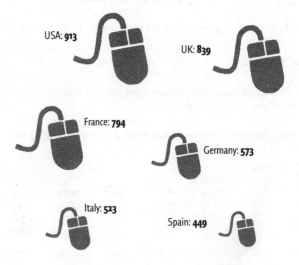

USA: **913**

UK: **839**

France: **794**

Germany: **573**

Italy: **523**

Spain: **449**

Not surprisingly, given the UK's love affair with computers, our take-up of broadband (**60%**) is considerably above average for developed nations

2008 was the year in which computer games became the most popular form of entertainment in Britain, with annual spending of an estimated **£4.64 billion** outstripping that on music and video (£4.46 billion)

ONLINE ENTERTAINMENT

The **top 10** websites for British users include Google, Facebook and Windows Live (the top 3), YouTube, eBay and Wikipedia

There are **3** porn sites in the top 50 websites

Digital sales of music – **8%** of the total music market – are higher than in any other European country except Spain. (In the USA the figure is almost a quarter)

Nearly **£1 in every £5** spent on UK advertising is for online adverts

BEING SOCIABLE

The most popular networking activity is uploading photos – **43%** of the population have done so

Percentage of the population who are members of a social networking site:

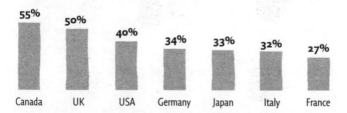

Canada	UK	USA	Germany	Japan	Italy	France
55%	50%	40%	34%	33%	32%	27%

Canadian enthusiasm for online social networking is partly due to the fact that the population is so thinly spread. The same does not apply to the UK ...

In 1996 the average Briton belonged to **6** organisations (such as churches, trade unions and neighbourhood societies)

In 2006 the average Briton belonged to **17** organisations, at least **8** of which were online communities

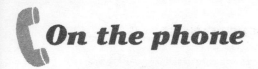

On the phone

GETTING IN TOUCH

By 1887 there were **26,000** telephones in use in Britain (compared to 150,000 in the United States in the same year)

By 1950, **1 in 10** households had a landline

By 2007, nearly **9 out of 10** households had a landline

THE INEXORABLE RISE OF THE MOBILE PHONE

Number of mobile phones in the UK:

📱📱📱📱📱📱📱📱📱

1998: **9 million**

📱📱📱📱📱📱📱📱📱📱📱📱📱📱📱📱📱📱
📱📱📱📱📱📱📱📱📱📱📱📱📱📱📱📱📱📱
📱📱📱📱📱📱📱📱📱📱

2004: **55 million**

📱📱📱📱📱📱📱📱📱📱📱📱📱📱📱📱📱📱
📱📱📱📱📱📱📱📱📱📱📱📱📱📱📱📱📱📱
📱📱📱📱📱📱📱📱📱📱📱📱📱📱📱📱📱📱
📱📱📱📱📱📱📱📱📱

2006: **69.6 million** (landline telephones: 33.6 million)

There are now more mobile phones than there are people in the UK

THE SAD DECLINE OF THE PAY PHONE

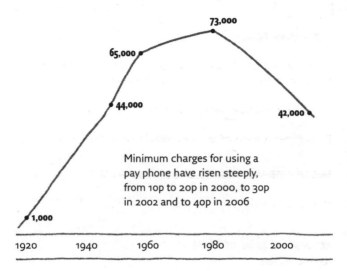

73,000

65,000

44,000

42,000

1,000

Minimum charges for using a
pay phone have risen steeply,
from 10p to 20p in 2000, to 30p
in 2002 and to 40p in 2006

1920   1940   1960   1980   2000

Around **2,000** red phone
boxes are listed buildings

9,000 have been saved by BT's 'adopt a kiosk'
scheme, which costs just **£1** per phone box

Keeping in touch

MAKING A CALL

A 2006 survey found that:

40% of men and **30%** of women have made telephone calls while naked

10% of people have put down the phone, leaving the other person talking to themselves

5% of people have found a telephone conversation so boring they have fallen asleep

In another survey **20%** of all complaints received by phone companies were from women reporting obscene calls from men

ESSENTIAL SERVICES

According to a *Guardian* article in 2007 the onset of the recession was having a significant impact on the pattern of enquiries to 118118. Comparing the first half of 2007 with the first half of 2008, it revealed that enquires about:

debt collection went up	**67%**
army recruitment went up	**60%**
second-hand shops went up	**299%**
pole and lapdancing outlets went up	**469%**

Calls to restaurants, on the other hand, were slightly down

THE JOY OF TEXT

Text messages sent per month per person in 2008:

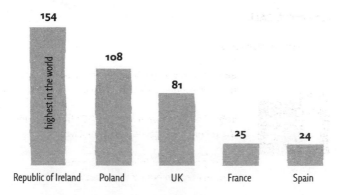

The 2007 ban on smoking in enclosed public areas
led to an increase in texting. Orange users sent
519.5 million during the fortnight after the ban,
compared with **512 million** during the fortnight before

> **Two-thirds** of people say they rely on their mobile phone or
> electronic organiser to remember key dates and numbers

As a result, **1 in 4** people cannot remember their own
landline telephone number, while **2 out of 3** can't recall
the birthdays of more than 3 friends or family members

THE JOY OF EMAIL

In 2008, **2 million** emails globally were sent every second.
Of these, around 160,000 were spam messages

DIY

The top **3** DIY internet searches in August 2008 were:

1 how to plaster
2 how to lay decking
3 how to hang wallpaper

A JOB WELL DONE – OR NOT

Bank Holidays traditionally are a peak time for DIY expenditure.
On August Bank Holiday in 2002, for example, it is estimated that
£400 million was shelled out on everything from paint to hammers

> **20%** of men claim that they can do
> DIY jobs better than any professional

Householders spend **£850 million** every year calling in
professionals to repair damage caused by botched DIY attempts

> Around **70** people are killed and
> **250,000** injured each year in DIY accidents

1 in 6 claims received by a leading insurer relate to DIY mistakes

---

The most common insurance claims include:

  pipe damage, from nails
  paint spillage
  ceiling damage from feet going through floor of the loft
  damage to prized ornaments
  fire damage caused by blow-torches/welders

One survey found that while **60%** of respondents claimed they could wire a plug, only **52%** could do so correctly

In 2003 the Department for Education and Skills found that **29%** of adults could not calculate the area of a floor, in either square feet or metres

More than **10%** were unable to understand the instructions on a packet of seeds

REGIONAL EXPERTISE

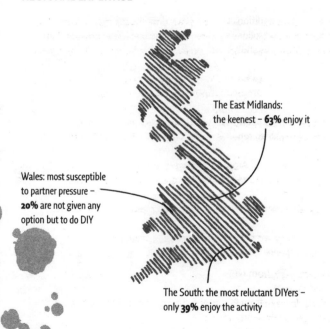

The East Midlands: the keenest – **63%** enjoy it

Wales: most susceptible to partner pressure – **20%** are not given any option but to do DIY

The South: the most reluctant DIYers – only **39%** enjoy the activity

Gardening

THE GREAT OUTDOORS

9 out of 10 people in Britain will spend over £10,000 maintaining a garden in their lifetime

Average daily time spent:

shopping **33 minutes**

gardening **29 minutes**

child care **25 minutes**

One survey found that **55%** of the population spend 2 or more hours a week gardening, while another found that 1 in 4 women prefer it to sex

Watching television programmes about gardening is nearly **10 times** more popular among people aged over 65 than it is among those aged 16–24

80% of people would rather have a barbecue as a family meal than a traditional dinner

NOT EVERYTHING IN THE GARDEN IS ROSY

A 2008 report estimated that in the previous 12 months:

1.2 million UK households had suffered a garden robbery

616,000 had suffered garden vandalism

420,000 had had items in their garden damaged by someone they knew

1 in 10 people are ashamed by the state of their neighbour's garden

1 in 5 think it could be 'vastly improved'

A survey of the **top 10** 'garden gripes' included barking dogs, neighbours arguing, half-finished building projects, topless sunbathing and wind chimes

5% of people have actually had a fight with a neighbour over a garden issue

5% have held a garden party and deliberately not invited their neighbours

3% have actively sabotaged a neighbour's garden (examples include damaging flowers or throwing litter over the fence)

Watering plants accounts for **6%** of our domestic water use

A 2002 survey asking people who they would most like to live next door to was topped by Alan Titchmarsh

Pets

43% of the population own a pet

60% of single people buy a pet for companionship,
39% of whom say they have replaced their partner with a pet

145,000 cats and dogs in the UK are on a vegetarian diet, while
16% of pet owners say they simply apply the government's advice (for
humans to eat 5 portions of fruit and vegetables a day) to their pet

21% of drivers have knocked down a cat or dog down while
driving; **25%** of these have driven off without reporting it

PURR-FECT COMPANIONS

The average cat costs its owner **£7,000** over its lifetime

Cats are on their way to overtaking dogs as the most popular pets
in the UK – there are **8 million** dogs and just over **8 million** cats

Back in 1979 there were a mere **4.9 million** pet cats

Cats are most popular with the 35–44 age group –
nearly a **third** of all people in this group own one.
Dogs tend to be preferred by older people

Nearly **2 out of 3** cat owners prefer to deal with
stress by curling up with their pet, saying it is more
effective than speaking to a friend or going for a drink

Almost **half** of cat owners in one survey said that they
would rather wake up with their cat than their partner

MAN'S BEST FRIEND

The average dog costs its owner **£20,000** over its lifetime

The most expensive breed is the Great Dane (**£31,840**), with an average lifespan of 10 years

The cheapest, despite a greater life expectancy of 12 years, is the Jack Russell (**£17,476**)

As of 2008 the Labrador Retriever is the most popular breed, followed by the Cocker Spaniel

83% of dog owners have no insurance for them

Annual distance covered:

The average gym member   **468 miles** (753km)

The average dog owner   **676 miles** (1,088km)

RABBITING ON

The average rabbit costs its owner **£4,000** over its lifetime

Rabbits are the **fourth** most popular pet after cats, dogs and fish

EXOTIC PETS

In a 2004 RSPCA survey of 300 pet shops that sold exotic animals, **81%** did not ask if the caller had prior experience of keeping the unusual pet in question. Almost **90%** failed to ask about the caller's family

Having a flutter

1999: **72%** of the population engaged in some form of gambling

2007: **68%** of the population engaged in some form of gambling

---

In 2007 the most popular forms of gambling were:

The National Lottery Draw **57%**
Scratchcards **20%**
Betting on horse races **17%**
Playing slot machines **14%**

Football and tennis are the most popular
sports to bet on, after horse racing

Only **6%** of people use the internet to gamble

There are around **4,000** bookmakers' permits
and **9,000** betting office licences in force in Great Britain

BACKING THE RIGHT HORSE

Over **6 million** people attended a
horse-racing meeting in Great Britain in 2003

The Grand National attracts over **10 million** UK viewers,
and another **600 million** worldwide

THE NATIONAL LOTTERY

70% of the adult population play the National Lottery on a regular basis, with an average weekly spend of around **£3**

> More than **2,200 millionaires** or multi-millionaires have been created

On the National Lottery TV show of 30 March 2007 it was announced that the amount raised for good causes since the Lottery's start in 1994 had passed the **£20 billion** mark

Where each £1 spent on the National Lottery goes:

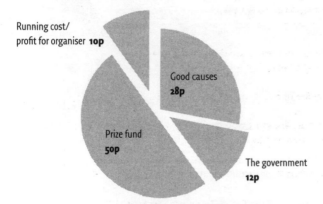

Running cost/
profit for organiser **10p**

Good causes
28p

Prize fund
50p

The government
12p

As of January 2006 there had been 24 unclaimed prizes in excess of £1 million. The highest was **£9,476,995**

> The average Briton is **176** times more likely to be murdered than to win the lottery with a single ticket

Minding our P's and Q's

PAST GLORIES

A 2009 study suggested that when the *Titanic* struck an iceberg in 1912, women with children had a **70%** better chance of surviving than men, because British men tended to queue politely for the lifeboats

RULES OF THE GAME

According to a report by the Future Foundation in 2002, **22%** of women would object to a man paying for dinner

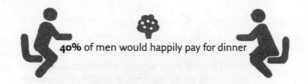

40% of men would happily pay for dinner

9 out of 10 women still like it if a man holds a door open for them

Most think it is 'ridiculous' for a man to stand up when a woman enters the room

PRESENT FAILINGS

A *Sunday Times* survey in 2000 found that **70%** of those questioned thought that society had got ruder over the previous 5 years

42% thought that rudeness was necessary 'to get your own way'

In 2002 an international survey revealed that Britons were 'the least wanted visitors around the world'. German tourists headed the politeness league, followed by the Japanese

1 in 4 of pupils excluded from Scottish schools in 2007 were guilty of verbally abusing teachers

Nearly **9 out of 10** UK drivers say that they have been the victims of road rage at least once

3 out of 5 drivers who admitted to road rage said they felt 'fine' about it and that the victims 'deserved it'

In **1 in 7** cases the aggressor actually got out of their car to abuse their victim verbally or physically

National sports

THE BEAUTIFUL GAME

Manchester United drew the highest average crowd in 2008/9 (**75,299**). Grays Athletic, on the other hand, attracted an average of 657 to each match

---

Top 5 premier league transfers:

1 Robinho: Real Madrid to Manchester City – **£32.5m** (2008)
2 Dimitar Berbatov: Tottenham to Manchester United – **£30.75m** (2008)
3 Andriy Shevchenko: AC Milan to Chelsea – **£30m** (2006)
4 Rio Ferdinand: Leeds to Manchester United – **£29.1m** (2002)
5 Juan Sebastian Veron: Lazio to Manchester United – **£28.1m** (2001)

The cheapest transfer is reckoned to be that of Tony Cascarino who transferred from Crockenhill FC to Gillingham FC in 1982 for a new strip and some training equipment

 The average cost of going to a football match in 2008–9, including travel, ticket, merchandise, food and drink, was **£95.60**, an increase of **20%** in 3 years

The biggest ever 'TV pick-up' was during the 1990 World Cup, after England's semi-final against West Germany. After the penalty shoot-out, demand soared to **2,800** megawatts, providing enough hot water for **3 million** cups of tea

28% of a football goal's area is considered 'unsaveable'

HOWZAT!

A study by the University of St Andrews of 418 England cricketers between 1876 and 1963 discovered that the more Tests played, the longer the player was likely to live, and that gentlemen 'amateurs' from privileged backgrounds tended to outlive professional cricketers

Odds against England winning the 2005 Ashes before the series started: **5–1**

After they lost the first match: **12–1**

Number of people who packed into Trafalgar Square when they won the series: **25,000**

Odds against England winning the 1981 Headingley Ashes Test when they were 135 for 7 following on, still nearly 100 runs short of making Australia bat again: **500–1**

Amount placed on England by Dennis Lillee and Rodney Marsh, 2 of the Australian players: **£15**

Amount they collected when Ian Botham and Bob Willis's miraculous performances won England the match: **£7,500**

To avoid being spotted betting against themselves, Lillee and Marsh got the driver of the Australian team bus to collect the winnings. They bought him a set of golf clubs, return air tickets to Australia and paid for his hotel

Tennis and other pursuits

TENNIS

According to the official website, the following quantities of food and drink are consumed during the fortnight of the Wimbledon Championship:

300,000 cups of tea and coffee
250,000 bottles of water
190,000 sandwiches
150,000 bath buns, scones, pasties and doughnuts
150,000 glasses of Pimm's
135,000 ice creams
100,000 pints of draught beer and lager
30,000 portions of fish and chips
28,000 kilograms (112,000 punnets) of English strawberries
22,000 slices of pizza
17,000 bottles of champagne
12,000 kilograms of poached and smoked salmon

GOLF

There are **2,500** golf courses in the UK. More than **800** of them have been built since the mid-1980s

2.5 million people play the game

1 in 4 of these is a manual worker

The most golf-inclined country in the world is the Republic of Ireland, where **7%** of the population belong to a club

DARTS

The 2009 Lakeside World Professional Championships Final
was watched by an average of **3.1 million**, with a peak of
4.5 million – **13%** of the entire viewing public

In 2007 one survey suggested that only **10%**
of regular pub-goers had played darts in the
last year, compared to **41%** in 2002

The survey also showed that **4 out of 10** men in their
twenties have never thrown a dart in their lives, and a
similar number have no idea what a bullseye is worth

Percentage of pubs with a dartboard in 2007: **53%**

SPORTY BRITAIN

Nearly **6 out of 10** adults in England don't participate
in 'moderate intensity sport' on any day of the week

90% of schools provide 2 hours of sports per week.
The government wants all schools to offer 5 hours per week by 2012

The number of girls taking a GCSE in PE increased by
34% between 2004 and 2007. This might be because
of the wider range of activities schools offer, since
competitive games stopped being compulsory for
14- to 16-year-olds in 2000

Dangerous sports

Fishing regularly tops lists of
the UK's most dangerous sport

1982: **11** people died while fishing
1998: **7** people died while fishing

Sports coming 2nd to fishing, with around
5 deaths per year each, include horse riding,
car racing and climbing

However, the sport with the highest number of injuries
per capita is rugby. Its players are **3 times** more likely to
get injured than those taking part in martial arts

Surveys rank boxing as a relatively safe sport:
in one survey it was the **53rd** most dangerous
sport, in another the **29th**

BOWLS

In 1999 a 70-year-old crown green
bowls player was banned for **2 years** by
the West Yorkshire County Bowls Association
after head-butting an opponent

SIX DEGREES OF DANGER

Insurance companies rank sports in categories, with category 6 being the most dangerous:

Category 6:
Bungee jumping, mountaineering over 15,000 feet (4,500 metres), powerboat racing, any professional sport

Category 5:
Hang-gliding, parachuting (other than BASE jumping), pot-holing, mountaineering up to 15,000 feet (4,500 metres), off-piste skiing, ice hockey

Category 4:
Scuba diving over 100 feet (30 metres)

Category 3:
Scuba diving to a maximum of 100 feet (30 metres), hot-air ballooning, skateboarding, white-water rafting

Category 2:
Amateur contact sport, e.g. hunting, fencing, boxing, martial arts, polo, rugby, soccer, mountain biking, parascending, high diving and jet-skiing

Category 1:
Non-contact sports, e.g. abseiling, motorcycle touring, yachting (inside territorial waters)

A trip to the cinema

45% of all UK cinema admissions occur in London

70% of Britain's cinema box office revenues are earned in London

UK cinema admissions in millions:

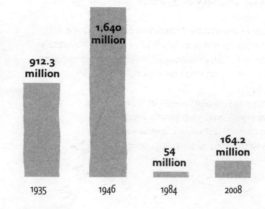

912.3 million	**1,640 million**	**54 million**	**164.2 million**
1935	1946	1984	2008

WHO GOES?

Nearly **50%** of the cinema audience for the top 20 films in 2007 were aged 24 or under

In 2007 **78%** of the audience for *Hairspray* was female; **72%** of the audience for *300* was male

While 2007's most popular film with white cinemagoers was *Harry Potter and the Order of the Phoenix*, the most popular with black, Indian and Pakistani audiences was *Shrek the Third*

WHAT DO THEY SEE?

5 top-earning films of all time in the UK:

1 *Mamma Mia!* 2008 **£69 million** | *Titanic* 1998 **£69 million**
3 *Harry Potter and the Philosopher's Stone* 2001 **£66 million**
4 *The Lord of the Rings: The Fellowship of the Ring* 2001 **£63 million**
5 *The Lord of the Rings: Return of the King* 2003 **£61 million**

THE POWER OF THE SILVER SCREEN

Asked to recall an advert seen on television for the first time the previous day, only **3%** of people can accurately describe it. However, among cinema audiences exposed to the same ad, accurate recall is **25%**

A 2001 survey of moviegoers found that nearly **half** had fallen asleep at the cinema, with nearly a **quarter** doing so in the preceding 3 months

Culture vultures

Proportion of the population making cultural visits in 2004:

Cinema: **61%**
Theatre: **24%**
Opera: **7%**
Ballet: **7%**
Art galleries: **24%**

In 2007 we spent **8 times** more on recreation and culture than we did in 1971

THEATRE AND ITS IRRITATIONS

A 2008 survey found that **52%** of theatregoers spent more than £200 per year on tickets

In a 2001 survey of theatregoers, **92%** said that they frequently found fellow audience members irritating, and **69%** said they had challenged someone about their behaviour. The most irritating habits recorded were:

Sweet wrapper rustling: **79%**
Talking and whispering: **69%**
Arriving late: **64%**
Mobile phone ringing: **59%**
Beeping of watches: **47%**

MUSEUMS AND ART GALLERIES

London has **7 of the 40** most-visited
museums and art galleries in the world

Tate Modern: **5.2 million visitors** (2007)
British Museum: **4.8 million**
National Gallery: **4.1 million**

It has been estimated that just over **4 in 10** of people
living in England visit a museum at least once a year

Damien Hirst's *For the Love of God*, a human skull made out of
platinum and diamonds, is the most expensive work of art ever
to have been created: the raw materials are worth **£12 million**

THE COST OF IT ALL

Top seats at ...

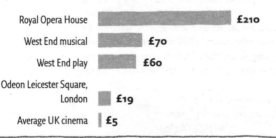

Royal Opera House	**£210**
West End musical	**£70**
West End play	**£60**
Odeon Leicester Square, London	**£19**
Average UK cinema	**£5**

Opera and jazz are equally popular,
but opera received **30 times** as much
public funding (£52 million) in 2007/8

The music scene

TOP OF THE POPS

The best-selling UK single is Elton John's double A-side 'Candle in the Wind 1997'/'Something About the Way You Look Tonight', which has sold nearly **5 million** in the UK

> In Channel 4's poll of 100 Greatest Number Ones, it came **third** in the category 'love to hate'

Number 2 spot on the best-seller list is taken by Band Aid's 1984 'Do They Know It's Christmas?' (**3.55 million** sales)

TOP UK ALBUMS OF ALL TIME

1 Queen: *Greatest Hits*
  (over **5.4 million** copies)
2 Beatles: *Sgt. Pepper's Lonely Hearts Club Band*
  (over **4.8 million** copies)
3 Oasis: *(What's the Story) Morning Glory*
  (over **4.3 million** copies)

Top 3 artists with most No.1 singles in the UK:

1 Elvis Presley: **21**
2 The Beatles: **17**
3 Cliff Richard: **14** | Westlife: **14**

Most-played songs in public places over the past 75 years:

1 Procol Harum: *A Whiter Shade of Pale*
2 Queen: *Bohemian Rhapsody*
3 Everly Brothers: *All I Have to Do is Dream*
4 Wet Wet Wet: *Love is All Around*
5 Bryan Adams: *(Everything I Do) I Do it for You*

Classical CDs accounted for **1 in 10** albums sold in the UK in 1990; they accounted for **1 in 20** in 2002

GETTING A MUSIC FIX

5% of the UK's total sales of albums – and **90%** of singles sales – are now digital downloads

The top 40 accounted for just **10%** of all UK single downloads in 2007

AND NOW ON RADIO ...

Total number of listeners in 2008:

BBC Radio 1 **10.6 million**

BBC Radio 2 **13.5 million**

BBC Radio 3 **2 million**

BBC Radio 4
9.9 million

BBC Radio FIVE LIVE **6 million**

90% of the population listen to the radio

Holidays and days out

THE BLACKPOOL PHENOMENON

The most popular holiday location in the UK is Blackpool

Blackpool is reputed to have more hotel and B&B beds than Portugal

Annual visitors in 1992 – **17 million**; in 2007 – **10 million**

Blackpool's illuminations use over **600 miles** of cable, and over **1 million** lamps

In 2001 the UK's most popular theme park (Blackpool Pleasure Beach) had more visitors (**6.5 million**) than the combined numbers for the top 5 churches and cathedrals (York Minster, Canterbury Cathedral, Westminster Abbey, Chester Cathedral and St. Paul's Cathedral)

It also beat the combined numbers for the top 5 historical houses and monuments (Tower of London, Edinburgh Castle, Windsor Castle, Roman Baths in Bath, Somerset House)

In 2007 the most popular attraction with free admission in England was Xscape Milton Keynes (featuring a mix of extreme sports, cinemas, restaurants etc), with **6.9 million** visitors

A SHORT BREAK

Butlin's opened their first holiday camp at
Skegness in 1936. At its peak the business was
catering for **2 million** holidaymakers each year

Now the UK's leading short-break holiday firm is Center Parcs;
they cater for **1.5 million** visitors each year. They operate in 5
countries (the Netherlands, Belgium, Germany, France and the
UK). In no language is the spelling of the firm's name correct

In 2008 the average Briton spent **£1,134** per person
on a holiday, compared with £1,380 on cigarettes,
soft drinks, snacks and newspapers

In 2001 an estimated **13.2%** of adults of working age and
7.5% of pensioners could not afford to take an annual holiday

CAMPING IT UP

The UK's Camping and Caravanning Club has reported
a **40%** increase in bookings in 2009, compared to 2008.
Its membership now stands at nearly half a million people

Half of the club's **top 10** most
popular campsites in the UK
are in the West Country

HONESTY TAKES A BREAK

Britons take home an estimated **430,000** gallons of shampoo
from hotels every year. This would fill **14,000** bathtubs. Other
stolen items mentioned in the survey that discovered this
included sewing kits, bathrobes and 'Do Not Disturb' signs

Only **19%** of guests felt guilty about taking the items

The Brits abroad

	1982	2006
Overseas holiday visits by UK residents	14,224,000	45,287,000
Spending	£2,477m	£23,300m
Trips abroad by sea	8,580,000	8,411,000
Trips by air	12,031,000	56,460,000

The total number of outward and inward trips made from UK's airports rose 100-fold between 1952 and 2007, from **1.5 million** to **150 million**

2008 showed a **3%** decline in the number of passengers

The number of Britons saying that they planned to spend their holidays in the UK **doubled** between 2008 and 2009

A 2008 survey found that **70%** of holidaymakers found it difficult to relax while abroad. **32%** of women worried about putting on weight because of their holiday eating

1 in 8 people have skived off work the first day they were due back after a holiday

WHERE DO WE GO

European destinations account for **80%** of UK residents' overseas trips. The most popular country for holidaymakers is consistently Spain (**13.8 million** visits in 2005), followed by France and Greece

The most popular non-European destination is
the USA; in 2003 it accounted for **5%** of holidays

In the mid-1960s, a flight to New York cost roughly **£200** –
approximately the same as it does today

PASSPORT CONTROL

Proportion of population holding passports:

Britain in 1984: **24%**

Britain today: **80%** of the population

USA today: **23%** of the population

Only **1** person in the UK is not required to have a passport – the
monarch. All other members of the Royal Family have one

VISITORS TO OUR SHORES

Top 5 nationalities visiting the UK in 2007:

1 USA (**3.56 million**)
2 France (**3.4 million**)
3 Germany (**3.37 million**)
4 Republic of Ireland (**2.97 million**)
5 Spain (**2.23 million**)

Cars

THE LONG AND WINDING ROAD

Great Britain's road network totals **248,968 miles** (400,675 kilometres). If stretched end to end, they would reach the moon

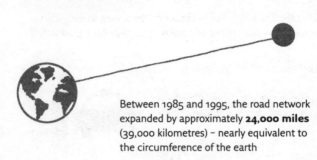

Between 1985 and 1995, the road network expanded by approximately **24,000 miles** (39,000 kilometres) – nearly equivalent to the circumference of the earth

2,189 miles (3,523 kilometres) are motorways, including 118 miles (190 kilometres) of the M25

France has **2 million** more cars than the UK's **25 million**, but its motorwork network is over **3 times** the size

145,864 miles (234,745 kilometres) of Britain's roads are unclassified (for instance, local streets)

In England, motorways account for less than **1%** of the total road length but carry nearly **20%** of traffic

There are **68** service stations on the motorway network

STUCK IN TRAFFIC

The UK has **6 of the 10** slowest moving cities in Europe.
In London in 2008 the average speed of traffic was
11.8 miles per hour – **40%** slower than Paris

> Newcastle-upon-Tyne fares rather better:
> the average speed there is **26.1 miles** per hour

One of the first recorded London traffic jams came in 1661 when
Samuel Pepys was held up in a Hackney carriage for **1.5 hours**

TAXI!

To travel 1 mile in London by black cab
typically costs between **£4.40** and **£8**

To travel 1 mile in Edinburgh by
Metrocab typically costs around **£3.80**

There are now more London cab drivers
over 70 than there are **under 30**

MADE IN THE UK

1922: Britain had **96** car-making firms

> 2007: it ranked **12th** in the list of top car producers,
> behind such countries as Brazil, Canada and Mexico

ROADKILL

> **273** hedgehogs are killed on British roads each day

Death on the roads

ACCIDENTS AND MISHAPS

In 1896 Bridget Driscoll became the first person to be killed by a car in the UK. The car was going at **4 miles per hour** (6.5 kilometres per hour)

In the same year Walter Arnold became the first person to receive a speeding ticket. He was fined 1 shilling for doing **8 miles per hour** (13 kilometres per hour) in a 2 miles per hour (3 kilometres per hour) zone

In 2007 **2,946** people died on the UK's roads – the lowest number since records began in 1928 (in the late 1920s up to 5,000 people were killed each year, even though car ownership then was the exception rather than the rule)

The lifetime risk of dying in a road accident has been estimated to be around **1 in 200**, with the equivalent figure for rail being **1 in 65,000** and for air **1 in 7.6 million**. Riders of motorbikes and mopeds are most at risk

WHY DO WE CRASH?

Drink:
16% of road deaths in 2007 occurred when the driver was over the legal limit. (The total for such deaths – 460 – was itself down from 560 the previous year)

Speed:
2005 Department of Transport figures revealed that exceeding the speed limit or going too fast for conditions were reported as a contributory factor in **15%** of all accidents. It was a contributory factor in **26%** of fatal accidents – 793 deaths

Bad driving:
In 2007 'failed to look properly' was the most frequently reported contributory factor in accidents, and **4 of the 5** most frequently reported contributory factors involved driver or rider error or reaction

THE GREAT SAT NAV HAZARD

A 2008 survey on Sat Nav systems found that:

> **1 in 10** drivers said the system had caused them to make an illegal turn

1 in 5 had lost track of traffic because they were distracted by it

> **1 in 4** had been sent the wrong way down a street by it

An estimated **300,000** accidents a year are caused by Sat Nav systems

Railways

THE EXPANDING NETWORK

In 1825 the first railway opened, between Stockton and Darlington

By 1851 **6,800** miles (10,900 kilometres) of track had been laid.
Speeds reached **60** miles per hour (97 kilometres per hour)

By 1900, **18,680** miles (30,060 kilometres) were in use.
Over **1,100 million** passengers were being carried every year

1950: British Railways' network peaked
at **21,000** miles (34,000 kilometres)

THE SHRINKING NETWORK

1963: Richard Beeching started his systematic
reduction of the network. **2,128** stations were closed

Today the network covers:

10,072 miles (16,309 kilometres) in Great Britain

189 miles (304 kilometres) in Northern Ireland

THE BUSIEST STATIONS

More trains pass through London's Clapham Junction railway station than any other station in Europe. At peak times **180** trains pass through per hour, of which 117 make a stop

The busiest station by number of entries and exits to the station is Waterloo (over **100 million** in the financial year 2007–8). The busiest train station in the world is Shinjuku Station in Tokyo – over 3.5 million people used it per day in 2007

Britain's top 10 busiest stations are all in London. The least busy station is Cross Keys in Wales, with only **8** passengers in 2007–8

HOW LATE IS LATE?

2007: First Great Western, operating the Bristol–London train service, was only obliged to record a train as 'late' if it was delayed by more than **10 minutes**. Almost **1 in 4** services were so delayed

Passengers on British Rail wasted **4,632 years** in 2001 as a result of late trains

In the same year, the average train on the 220-mile (350-kilometre) line linking Tokyo, Nagoya and Osaka was late by **18 seconds**

HOW OVERCROWDED IS OVERCROWDED?

In 2008 the Department of Transport announced that it was countering the problem of overcrowding on trains by changing the definition of 'overcrowding'. Instead of **10** standing passengers per 100 seated, a train would now require **30** standing per 100 seated to be classed as overcrowded

The most overcrowded service in 2008 was the 07.15 from Cambridge to London King's Cross, with **76** passengers standing for every 100 seated

Air travel

THE FIRST TO FLY

Imperial Airways was the first sizeable firm offering commercial air travel. It was formed in March 1924 from the merger of 4 smaller companies

---

In the first year of operation the company:

flew **853,042** miles (1,372,838 kilometres)
carried **11,395** passengers
carried **212,380** letters

In April 1925, they showed the first in-flight movie (*The Lost World* on the London–Paris route). 2 years later they became the first airline to offer passengers cooked meals

In 1934 a flight from London to Paris took **3** hours. Today it takes about **1** hour

Concorde flew so fast that the weight of everyone onboard was temporarily reduced by about **1%** when flying east. This was due to the centrifugal effect of the airspeed added to the rotation speed of the Earth. Flying west, people's weight increased by about **0.3%**

HEATHROW AIRPORT

Heathrow is the 3rd busiest passenger airport in the world. In 2007 it dealt with **68,068,304** passengers. The busiest was Hartsfield-Jackson Atlanta International Airport (89,379,287) and 2nd was Chicago O'Hare (76,177,855)

The airport is **6 times** the size of Monaco

Heathrow Airport has **7** chaplains (Anglican, Catholic, Free Church, Jewish, Muslim, Hindu and Sikh)

In 2007 British Airways lost **2.65** bags for every 100 passengers

900 laptops are lost there each week

10% of Britain's perfume sales take place there

THE STRESSES OF TRAVEL

In 2003 Manchester Airport surveyed its passengers to ask how they could improve their Christmas service. **40%** of respondents replied 'by not playing "Merry Christmas Everybody" by Slade'. The airport duly dropped the song from its playlist

Bicycles

THE RISE OF THE BIKE

The first mechanically-propelled 2-wheel vehicle is believed to have been built by Kirkpatrick MacMillan, a Scottish blacksmith, in 1839. In 1842 he was arrested and fined for knocking over a child when riding on the pavement

By the 20th century, bicycles were becoming increasingly popular. As late as 1950, they were used for travelling around **12.5 billion** miles (20 billion kilometres) on the road – more than a quarter of all road mileage

Today, bicycles are responsible for less than **1%** of the total distance travelled by road

Around **3.5 million** bicycles were sold in 2005

The percentage of households owning at least 1 bicycle has risen from **36%** in 1989–91 to **47%** in 2002–3. The number of bicycles owned has increased from 29 per 100 people to 38 per 100 during the same period

In 2007 over **9 million** trips were made to school on the National Cycle Network

COMING A CROPPER

In 1950 **1** cyclist died for every **15.5 million** miles (25 million kilometres) travelled. In 2005, the figure was **1** for every **18.5 million** miles (30 million kilometres). In the same period, the amount of traffic on Britain's roads (excluding motorways) rose by **700%**

Over **480,000** journeys are made by bicycle in London every day. Since 2000, cycling levels in London have increased by **83%**. The number of cyclists killed or seriously injured has fallen by **31%**. However, **8 to 12** cyclists are killed as a result of collisions with Heavy Goods Vehicles every year

90% of accidents occur in urban areas (where **77%** of cycling takes place)

75% occur at or near a road junction

 80% occur in daylight

80% of cyclist casualties are male

In 2005–6, **439,000** bicycles were stolen. This equates to 1 being stolen every 71 seconds. Although this is a **10%** rise on the previous year, it is still **34%** below the 1995 peak

The UK Tandem Club has over **5,000** members

Fashion-conscious Britain

IT'S WHAT'S ON THE INSIDE THAT COUNTS

*Proportion of people believing clothes have
no bearing on how they are perceived:*

Men: **43%**
Women: **19%**

64% of women find shopping for clothes a 'depressing' experience.
10% have cried in a changing room

Average time spent looking at an expensive
item of clothing before buying: **22** minutes

Average time spent looking at a house
or flat before buying: **18** minutes

2 out of 3 new mothers in London spend more
on their children's clothes than on their own

FASHION STATEMENTS

Worst fashion items of all time (2007 survey amongst women):

1 Shell suit
2 Poncho
3 Leg warmers
4 Clogs
5 Braces

And the best:

1 Jeans
2 Black dress
3 Mini skirt
4 Bikini
5 Knee-high boots

MADE-UP FOR THE OCCASION

Women in the UK spend about
£1.2 billion a year on make-up

In one survey **64%** of company directors said that
women who wore make-up looked more professional

18% said that women who do not wear make-up
'look like they can't be bothered to make an effort'

BODILY ADORNMENTS

10% of people have a body piercing other than on their
earlobe. Amongst 16–24-year-old girls, that figure is **46%**

1 in 6 women have a tattoo

1 in 10 men have a tattoo. (Tattoos have a venerable
history: King Harold had a tattoo ('Edith' – the name of
his mistress – and 'England', over his heart). Former Prime
Minister James Callaghan had one on his arm; it was for
this reason that he never wore short-sleeved shirts)

The nation's wardrobe

WOMEN

The average dress size in Britain is **16**

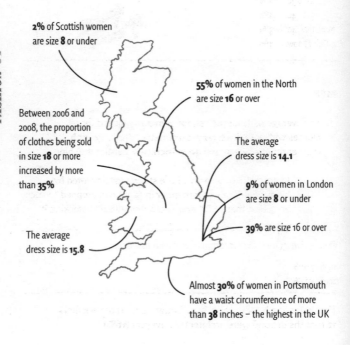

2% of Scottish women are size **8** or under

55% of women in the North are size **16** or over

Between 2006 and 2008, the proportion of clothes being sold in size **18** or more increased by more than **35%**

The average dress size is **14.1**

9% of women in London are size **8** or under

39% are size 16 or over

The average dress size is **15.8**

Almost **30%** of women in Portsmouth have a waist circumference of more than **38** inches – the highest in the UK

The average woman has more than **100** items of clothing in her wardrobe, but wears fewer than **a third** of them regularly

On average, women keep their favourite piece of clothing for **12** years. The average length of marriage is **11.5** years

How many pairs of shoes do you own?

1 to 10:	**50%**
11 to 20:	**30%**
21 to 30:	**11%**
31 to 40:	**4%**
More than 40:	**3%**
Don't know:	**1%**

MEN

The average male clothes shopper in 2004 looked for clothes with a **42-inch** (107-centimetre) chest, **37-inch** (94-centimetre) waist and **40.5-inch** (102-centimetre) hips

In 2007 the popularity of the string vest (invented by a Norwegian army commander in 1933) had dropped to such an extent that ASDA and Tesco discontinued stocking it

Proportion of men in professional jobs who buy ties:

1996: **70%**
2006: **56%**

The profession least likely to have bought a tie in the previous 12 months in 2006 were architects/surveyors (**16%**)

Men have an average of **9** items which they haven't worn during the past year

Underwear

LET'S KEEP THIS BRIEF ...

The Rational Dress League, founded in 1898 to campaign against overly formal attire, called for women to wear no more than **7 pounds** of underwear

Most popular colour for men purchasing lingerie as a gift for their partner: black (**33%**)

Proportion of women who prefer that colour for themselves: **29%**

The most popular colour with women is cream/white (**32%**)

16% of men choose red. Only **7%** of women would like to receive that colour

80% of women who have received lingerie as a gift claim they liked and have worn it

The average woman owns **22** pairs of knickers

18% of British women have gone to work without wearing knickers. Only **8%** of French women have done the same

Y-FRONTS OR BOXERS?

Y-fronts first went on sale in the UK in 1938. Their popularity swiftly became such that at the 1948 Olympics, every member of the British team was given a pair

Boxer shorts are now the most popular men's underwear at Marks & Spencer, although hipster trunks are gaining ground

HOW CLEAN IS YOUR UNDERWEAR?

12% of people in London own a pair of underpants or knickers that are more than 10 years old

Nationwide, more than **1 in 10** people admit to wearing the same pair of pants more than **3 days** in a row

4% of men have gone a whole week without changing their pants

5% of people have turned pants inside out to get an extra day's wear

19% of men have sprayed pants with aftershave to mask their smell

WHAT SCOTTISH MEN WEAR UNDER THEIR KILTS

69% – nothing
14% – boxer shorts
10% – briefs
7% – 'other'

Eating in

WHAT DO WE EAT?

Items included in the 'basket of goods' used to calculate the Retail Prices Index and therefore regarded as 'typical' of British diet:

1947

Large and small white loaves
Rolled oats
Flank (cut of beef)
Mutton, lamb breast
Wild rabbits
Hake, frozen cod fillets
Compound cooking fat
Condensed milk
Turnips
Swede
Prunes
Canned plums

1962

Sliced white bread
Small brown loaf
Cream crackers, crispbread
Brisket, silverside, rump steak
Tinned stewed steak
Luncheon meat
Fish fingers
Cheese spread
Crisps
Mushrooms
Frozen and canned peas
Canned pears

1987

Spaghetti
Rice pudding
Mince, beefburgers
Turkey
Garlic sausage
Trout, mackerel, salmon
Cod in sauce
Cooking oil
Regional cheese
Frozen chips
Peanuts
Frozen curry and rice, frozen pizza
Tinned ravioli

2005

Large wholemeal loaf, pitta bread
Muesli
Pasta
Rump steak, braising steak,
mince, topside
Frozen chicken nuggets
Canned tuna
Margarine, low-fat spread
Selected speciality cheeses
Flavoured milk
Fromage frais
Pre-packed salads
Kiwi fruit

BAKED BEANS AND OTHERS

The British consume at least **twice as many** baked beans per person as any other nationality

In 1978 average yoghurt consumption was just **45ml** per person per week

In 2006 this figure had risen to **204ml**

Of the **100 million** pots of yoghurt and yoghurt drinks sold each week, more than **9 million** are thrown away unopened

Pot Noodles were launched in Lancashire in 1979. By 2003 **5.5** pots were being sold per second, and the manufacturers had more than 50 student brand managers promoting the snack at universities

LUXURY FOOD

August 2008 list of the most expensive foods available (prices per kilo):

1 Gold (leaf used to decorate luxury dishes) (£17,000–£60,000)
2 Almas caviar (£10,000–£18,000)
3 White truffles (£1,600–£5,000)
4 Bird's nest soup (£1,000–£5,000)
5 Saffron (£580–£5,800)

A NON-MEAT DIET

In today's Britain **1 in 17** households has at least 1 vegetarian, while **3%** of the population are 'completely' vegetarian

Research published in the British Medical Journal in 2006 suggested that, on average, vegetarians had an IQ **5 points** above those who regularly eat meat

Eating out

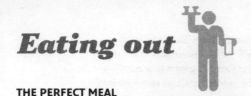

THE PERFECT MEAL

1932, ABC restaurant (a popular chain)

***

Thick mock turtle soup
Roast ribs of beef and Yorkshire pudding,
boiled potatoes, spring greens
Bread-and-butter pudding or a roll and cheese

The total cost was 1s 6d (7.5p)

1947, ideal meal according to a Gallup poll

***

Tomato soup
Sole
Roast chicken with roast potatoes,
peas and sprouts
Trifle and cream
Cheese and biscuits

1973, equivalent poll

***

Tomato soup or prawn and shrimp cocktail
Steak with roast potatoes or chips, peas,
sprouts and mushrooms
Trifle or apple pie and cream
Cheese and biscuits

More recently, curry has become king. In 1950 there were only **6** Indian restaurants in Britain; by 2004 their number had grown to around **9,000** (twice the number of Chinese restaurants)

The Food Standards Agency estimates that Indian restaurants account for **two-thirds** of all eating out in the UK

Chicken tikka masala was invented in Britain to appease domestic tastes, and now accounts for **1 in 7** curries sold in the UK. There seems to be no standard recipe. A 1998 survey of **48** restaurants found that the only common ingredient in their chicken tikka masalas was chicken

According to a *Daily Telegraph* survey in 2008, **£1 in every £100** is spent in a fish and chip shop. Around **276 million** fish and chip meals are sold each year from almost 10,500 shops

Restaurants

WHERE DO WE GO?

In 2005 the UK had **26,416** restaurants, and they served **734 million** meals at a value of **£5.27 billion** (or **£7.61 billion** when drinks were included)

In 2003 **22%** of Britain's restaurants were in London

THE BEST

The Michelin Guide: Great Britain and Ireland 2009 gives its much-coveted 3 stars to **3** restaurants in Britain: The Fat Duck (Bray, Berkshire), Restaurant Gordon Ramsay (London), The Waterside Inn (Bray)

In 2006 the *Independent* rated the Restaurant Gordon Ramsay as the most expensive in London. A meal there, including tip and 1 alcoholic drink, was said to cost **£108** per person

TIPPING

A 2008 survey found that more than **half** of diners usually leave tips of **10%** or more; **1 in 5** people tipped about **5%**, even if the service had been good

49% wouldn't demand removal of a service charge, even if the service had been bad. **24%** left an extra tip on top of a service charge

People in Scotland are the most frequent tippers, with **55%** always leaving one. Those in the north of England are the least likely to leave a tip

RESTAURANT ETIQUETTE

2006 survey of young professionals in London:

71% said they would not order dishes in restaurants if they thought there was a risk of their mispronouncing the name

65% had chosen food or wine during business lunches based upon a desire to impress others rather than because it was what they wanted

63% said they would rather accept unsatisfactory food in silence than cause a scene by sending it back

Half of the restaurants and catering establishments inspected by the Food Standards Agency in 2000 had broken one or more food safety rules

Each year around **4.5 million** people in England go down with food poisoning

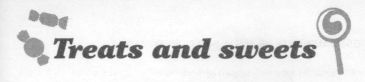

Treats and sweets

SWEET-TOOTHED BRITAIN

A 2008 survey found that the average person in the UK consumes more than **8.3 million** calories in their lives in the form of unhealthy snacking, equivalent to 10 years of the recommended daily intake of calories for adults

The average person each week scoffs **3** chocolate bars, **3** packets of crisps, **1** cereal bar, **1** bag of nuts, **1** muffin, **4** biscuits and **6** sweets

CHOCAHOLICS UK

Chocolate consumption per capita, 2003:

Switzerland **22.5 pounds** (10 kilograms)

Austria **20 pounds** (9 kilograms)
Republic of Ireland **19.5 pounds** (9 kilograms)
Germany **18 pounds** (8 kilograms)

UK **17.5 pounds** (8 kilograms)

Australia **13 pounds** (6 kilograms)
USA **11.5 pounds** (5 kilograms)
Italy **6 pounds** (3 kilograms)
Japan **4 pounds** (2 kilograms)

Spain **3.5 pounds** (1.5 kilograms)

OUR FAVOURITE TREATS: A BRIEF CHRONOLOGY

1882 Smarties (originally known as 'Chocolate Beans'. The prefix 'Smarties' was added in 1937. In 1977 Rowntree's were forced to drop the name 'Chocolate Beans' by trading standards authorities, on the grounds that it was misleading)

1905 Cadbury's Dairy Milk bar (in some estimates, the best-selling chocolate bar in the UK)

1924 Milky Way (with a very low density of 0.88g/cubic cm, a Milky Way bar will float in water)

1930 Marathon (it changed its name to Snickers in 1990. This is the title by which it had always been known in the USA, having been named after one of the Mars family's favourite horses)

1932 Mars

1936 Maltesers

1967 Twix (originally called Raider in many countries)

1981 Wispa (originally costing 16p. It was withdrawn from sale in 2003, but after campaigns on social networking websites such as Facebook and MySpace, Cadbury's reintroduced it in 2008)

1991 Green & Black's first organic chocolate bar

A NATION OF CRISP-MUNCHERS

The British eat **10 billion** packets a year – more than half of all crisps sold in the European Union

Walkers Crisps' Leicester site uses **800** tons of potatoes per day to make **10 million** bags of crisps, making it the UK's largest grocery brand

Soft drinks

A NICE HOT BREW

These days, the British drink **165 million** cups of tea a day –
around 3 cups a day for every man, woman and child.
While we account for a mere **0.91%** of the world's population,
we are responsible for **6%** of its tea consumption

95% of the UK population uses tea bags

98% add milk

45% add sugar

Sales of herbal and fruit tea rose by **30%** from 2002–4, and sales of
speciality varieties, such as green tea, increased by over **50%**. During
the same period, sales of traditional tea bags decreased by **16%**

Coffee maintains its popularity, to the tune of **70 million** cups
consumed per day. **72%** of British people drink it regularly. In
some regions (such as the Northeast) it is the most frequently
consumed beverage, drunk almost twice as often as tea

85% of UK coffee drinkers take milk in their coffee

57% add sugar

According to a 2008 survey, **one-third** of UK office workers
take tea and coffee breaks at work to alleviate boredom

1 in 5 admit to making tea and coffee for colleagues
in order to climb the career ladder

In Sheffield **1 in 3** people drink more than **6** cups of tea a day

More office workers personalise their workspace with a tea or
coffee mug than with photographs or other personal items

POSH WATER

Up until the 1980s the idea of buying bottled water was a very foreign idea to most British people. In 1980 only **25 million** litres were consumed – under half a litre per person per year

By 2006 bottled water was a **£1,700 million** business, with each of us consuming **38** litres a year

However, UK bottled water consumption remains well behind the West European average of **110** litres

Average daily consumption:

3 cups of tea

1 coffee

Half a glass of mineral water

Hard liquor

WHAT'S YOUR POISON?

Traditionally, we have been a nation of beer and spirits drinkers. In the late 19th century average annual consumption of wine was a mere **0.4** gallons per person (1.8 litres, or **14.5 small glasses**) – less than half that of spirits, which was **1.04** gallons (4.7 litres or **118 shots**) and a long way behind beer consumption, which was **31.4** gallons (142.7 litres or just over **251 pints**)

In the 2nd half of the 20th century, the story changed

Units of alcohol consumed annually, per head 1950–1:

Beer **337**

Wine **13**

Spirits **103**

Total **453**

Units of alcohol consumed annually, per head 2000–1:

Wine **228**

Beer **400**

Spirits **159**

Total **787**

In the 25 years leading up to 2003, beer consumption fell by **20%**; that of wine grew by **260%**

THE RISE OF WINE

The heartiest wine fans are women, whose consumption of wine rose **27%** in the 5 years to 2003. In that year females accounted for **55%** of the UK wine market, compared with **24%** of the beer market

Despite this trend, however, we still lag behind our continental counterparts. Each Briton averaged **17** litres of wine in 2003 (it had been 14 litres in 1998), but the Italians averaged **47.5** litres, and the French **49** litres

---

Total UK consumer expenditure, 2006:

£19 billion on beer
£14.5 billion on wine
£7.8 billion on spirits

Lager accounts for **85%** of all beer sales

THE DECLINE OF THE LOCAL

In 2005–6, of the average weekly household expenditure on alcoholic drink of **£14.80**, £8.50 was spent in licensed premises, and £6.30 in off-licences (including supermarkets)

In 1998 **30%** of beer was bought in shops and supermarkets. 10 years later, that figure had become **41%**

In 2008 pubs were closing at the rate of **5 a day**

Drinking to excess?

ARE WE A NATION OF ALCOHOLICS?

The average weekly consumption for men is **18.7** units – just over twice the level for women

Drinking habits of men and women in 2006:

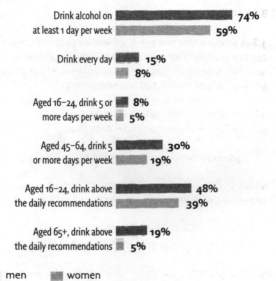

Drink alcohol on at least 1 day per week: **74%** / **59%**

Drink every day: **15%** / **8%**

Aged 16–24, drink 5 or more days per week: **8%** / **5%**

Aged 45–64, drink 5 or more days per week: **30%** / **19%**

Aged 16–24, drink above the daily recommendations: **48%** / **39%**

Aged 65+, drink above the daily recommendations: **19%** / **5%**

men   women

People in 'professional or managerial' households drink **15.1** units per week (just over 15 small glasses of wine) – more than any other type of household. Those in 'routine and manual' households drink **11.6** units

People in Scotland drink **11.6** units every week – in England it's **13.7** units, in Wales **13.5** units

In 2004 in the UK as a whole **61%** of people had heard of the government guidelines on alcohol intake. Of these people, more than **a third** said that they did not know what the recommendations were

The number of alcohol-related deaths in the UK more than doubled between 1991 and 2007 (**8,724**)

Britons still drink less alcohol per head than the French, Germans or Spanish

BINGE BRITAIN?

53,844 people under the age of 25 were admitted to English hospitals in 2006–7 for alcohol-related reasons. Alcohol is blamed for more than 500,000 hospital admissions of all ages each year, as well as over half a million crimes

The rate of alcohol-related admissions to hospital rises sharply between **midnight** and **5am** every day

360,000 11–15-year-olds get drunk every week

4 million men and **1.9 million** women binge drink (drink more than twice the recommended daily guidelines on some occasions)

In the UK, binge drinking accounts for **40%** of all drinking occasions by men and **22%** of those by women

But heavy drinking is not a new phenomenon. In the early 18th century **1 in every 4** houses in London's Westminster and St Giles were said to be selling gin. In the 1740s people in England were drinking an annual **2.2** gallons (10 litres) of gin each

Alcohol consumption at the turn of the 20th century was over **10** litres of pure alcohol per person per year (compared to **9** litres now; the figure dropped to **4** litres in the 1930s)

Mr and Mrs average

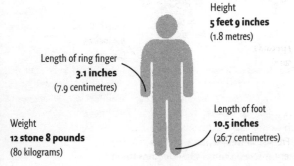

Average British man 2002:

Height
5 feet 9 inches
(1.8 metres)

Length of ring finger
3.1 inches
(7.9 centimetres)

Weight
12 stone 8 pounds
(80 kilograms)

Length of foot
10.5 inches
(26.7 centimetres)

The average British man is **1 inch** (2.5 centimetres) taller than his French counterpart, but shorter than the average Dutchman by **0.2 inches** (0.5 centimetres) – the Dutch are now the tallest nation in the world

Average British woman 2002:

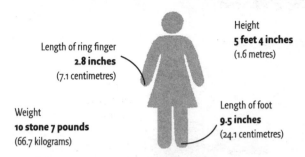

Height
5 feet 4 inches
(1.6 metres)

Length of ring finger
2.8 inches
(7.1 centimetres)

Weight
10 stone 7 pounds
(66.7 kilograms)

Length of foot
9.5 inches
(24.1 centimetres)

British women are fractionally taller
than French women, but **0.1 inches**
(0.3 centimetres) shorter than Dutch women

The average height seems to have risen over time
as diet has improved. One estimate of heights in
the 17th century suggested that men were, on
average, **5 feet 6 inches** (1.7 metres) and women
were **5 feet 0.5 inches** (1.5 metres). This seems to
have remained virtually unchanged until Victorian times

Expanding waistlines

A BIGGER SPREAD: WOMEN

Average UK woman:

	Height	Weight	Waist	Hips
1951	**5ft 2in** (1.6m)	**9st 10lbs** (61.7kg)	**27in** (69cm)	**39in** (99cm)
2001	**5ft 4in** (1.6m)	**10st 3lbs** (64.9kg)	**34in** (86cm)	**40in** (102cm)

As of 2002, British women are on average heavier than all other nationalities except Americans

The British female bottom is **34 inches** (83 centimetres) – 2 inches (5 centimetres) behind the female Italian bottom, which is the largest in the world

Average clothes size: **16**

Average bra size **36C** (as compared with **34B** in the late 1990s)

In 2007 Marks & Spencer's made larger bras available. Their previous biggest size was **G**, but they now added GG, H, HH and J

Average shoe size **6**

A BIGGER SPREAD: MEN

Between 1995 and 2005 the average weight for a man increased by 7.7 pounds (3.5 kilograms) to **12 stone 13 pounds** (82.1 kilograms)

> A 2006 survey found the UK to be one of the heaviest nations in Europe. Its average Body Mass Index (weight in relation to height) was **25.4**. (The World Health Organisation say that **18.5–25** is healthy, **25–30** is overweight)

Slimmest: Italy: **24.3**
Heaviest: Malta: **26.6**

Barry Austin, Britain's heaviest man, once weighed **65 stone** (412.8 kilograms). From this peak (in his late 20s), he slimmed down to 45 stone (285.8 kilograms) by the age of 38 (in 2006). The 5 feet 11 inches (1.8 metres) tall man from Birmingham cited a typical day's intake (before his diet) as:

3 English breakfasts
2 portions of fish and chips
3 roast dinners
1 family-sized trifle
17 litres of cola

Total: **29,000** calories

Fat Britain

FAT ADULTS

It is estimated that by 2010 **13 million** Britons – nearly **1 in 4** – will be obese. At present slightly more women (**24.3%**) than men (**22.1%**) are clinically obese

In 2008 Shetland was identified as the region with the most obese people (**15.5%** registered with their GP as obese), followed by Torfaen (**13.9%**) and Blaenau Gwent (**12.5%**)

The highest percentage (over **65%**) of women with a waist size of more than 32 inches is to be found in Sheffield

The 'thinnest' areas of Britain are all in London, with Camden leading the way, followed by Richmond and Twickenham, and Kensington and Chelsea

Between 1997 and 2003 cases of diabetes (which can be linked to obesity) rose by **74%** in the UK

FAT CHILDREN

Nearly **1 in 6** children aged between 2 and 10 is now clinically obese

> More than **8 out 10** obese children
> remain obese into adulthood

In 2006 **1 in 3** boys aged 11–15 from low-income families
did no sports or exercise at all in the week prior to interview.
For boys from high-income families the figure was **1 in 5**

NOT JUST THE BRITS

According to the World Health Organisation,
the 3 most obese nations are:

1 Nauru
2 Micronesia
3 Cook Islands

> The USA comes in at number **9**, and the UK is
> sandwiched between Andorra and Saudi Arabia at **28**

TAKING STEPS

4,000 men in 2006 had their 'man boobs' or 'moobs' removed

> **85%** of women worry about their body every day;
> **46%** say that if they had a better body they would
> change career, while **12%** would change partner

> **17%** of children (aged 5–15) consume
> 5 or more portions of fruit and veg a day

30% of adult women eat 5 or more fruit and veg per day; **26%** of men

Illnesses and accidents

A HISTORY OF SICKNESS

Records of causes of death in earlier periods are often vague, but the following figures, taken from London parish records for 1700, show that infectious disease probably used to be the biggest killer:

Convulsion	**4,631**
Ague (malaria or other diseases involving chills)	**3,676**
Consumption and tissick (cough)	**2,819**
Smallpox, measles etc	**1,031**

It has been estimated that up to **50%** of deaths were the result of infectious diseases such as TB, cholera and typhoid in mid-Victorian times

THE HEALTH OF THE NATION

Top 5 reasons for visits to the doctor in 2005:

1 Hypertensive diseases
2 Dermatitis and eczema
3 Other skin disorders
4 Upper-respiratory infections
5 Eye disorders

Top 5 causes of death in 2005:

1 Circulatory system diseases
2 Cancer
3 Respiratory diseases
4 Digestive diseases
5 Accident etc

Breast and lung cancer cases have doubled over the past 30 years, but this has much to do with the fact that life expectancy overall has risen – cancer tends to affect older people

Between 1991 and 2007 the number of anti-depressant prescriptions dispensed in England nearly quadrupled to **34 million**

WHOOPSY-DAISY

The British Home Accident Surveillance Report for 2001 included the following entries:

More than **3,000** people were taken to casualty after falling over laundry baskets

Emergency hospital treatment needed due to accidents involving ...

tea cosies	**40**
clogs	**300**
place mats	**165**
dustpans	**146**
bread bins	**91**

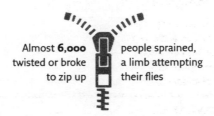

Almost **6,000** people sprained, twisted or broke a limb attempting to zip up their flies

Glossy magazines caused **4** times more accidents than chainsaws

Teeth 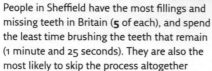 and eyes

TEETHING TROUBLES

People in Sheffield have the most fillings and missing teeth in Britain (**5** of each), and spend the least time brushing the teeth that remain (1 minute and 25 seconds). They are also the most likely to skip the process altogether

The country's best teeth are to be found in Brighton, where people have an average of just **2** fillings and **2** missing teeth

 In Portsmouth, **29%** of people never go to the dentist. In York the figure is **14%**

People in Southampton have the worst breath, while those in Birmingham have the best

CHEW ON THIS

In 1999 Tony Blair promised that everyone would have access to an NHS dentist

In March 2007 **2 million** patients who wanted an NHS dentist were still unable to find one

---

Proportion of dentists' income coming from private (as opposed to NHS) work:

1990: **6%**
2004–5: **52.4%**

Average cost of a standard filling, 2008:

UK – most expensive in Europe: **€156**
Hungary – least expensive in Europe: **€8**

Of the **77,000** British people who went abroad in 2006 for medical treatment, an estimated **43%** went for dental care

SIGHT UNSEEN

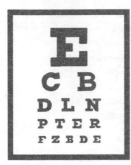

Between a **third** and a **quarter** of the population are short-sighted

Approximately **3 million** wear contact lenses

A 2004 survey conducted eyesight tests on people who did not wear glasses. **65%** of those who failed were drivers

1 in 3 of those who failed admitted they had suspected their sight was not perfect

Surveys show that there is absolutely no link between the wearing of glasses and high intelligence

The NHS

A MIGHTY ARMY

The National Health Service employs more than **1.3 million** people. Of those, just under half are clinically qualified, including:

90,000 hospital doctors

35,000 GPs

400,000 nurses

16,000 ambulance staff

Only the Chinese People's Liberation Army, the Wal-Mart supermarket chain and the Indian Railways directly employ more people

In 2002–3, the NHS's budget was increased by **£5.2 billion**

Nearly **one-third** of this went on pay increases to attract and retain staff

Of the NHS's total budget for 2002–3 of **£55 billion**, **55%** went on staff costs

PROBLEMS ON THE WARD

The number of NHS beds in England
halved between 1980 and 2005

More people are killed each year by
MRSA (an infection which can be contracted
in hospital) than by road accidents

Nevertheless, in a 2008 survey, **82%** of people said they were proud
of the NHS, while **51%** agreed that it was still the envy of the world

DIAL 999

The 999 emergency number is called **80,000** times
per day, the busiest time being between 10.30pm and
midnight (around **6,000** calls per hour), and the busiest
day is New Year's Day (up to **12,000** calls per hour)

Some of the less urgent enquiries have been from:

a man who couldn't find his trousers

a woman who had been splashed
by a car driving through a puddle

a caller who had spotted a mysterious light in
the night-time sky; it turned out to be the moon

Cosmetic surgery

PLASTIC FANTASTIC?

The UK cosmetic surgery industry was worth **£359 million** in 2005.
It grew by **242%** between 2000 and 2005

In that year **2%** of the population had work done.
A further **16%** of UK consumers said they would consider surgery

---

Cosmetic surgical procedures carried out in 2008 by members of BAAPS (The British Association of Aesthetic Plastic Surgeons):

On women: **31,183**
On men: **3,004**

UNDER THE KNIFE

Breast augmentation is the most popular procedure for women in the UK. The number of breast augmentation procedures carried out by members of BAAPS rose from 2,361 in 2002 to **6,497** in 2007

3,638 abdominoplasty procedures ('tummy tucks') were carried out in 2008 – a rise of **30%** from 2007

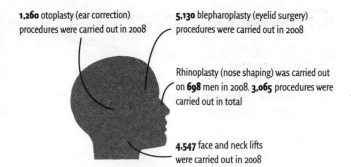

1,260 otoplasty (ear correction) procedures were carried out in 2008

5,130 blepharoplasty (eyelid surgery) procedures were carried out in 2008

Rhinoplasty (nose shaping) was carried out on **698** men in 2008. **3,065** procedures were carried out in total

4,547 face and neck lifts were carried out in 2008

There was only a very slight increase in teenagers expressing interest in cosmetic surgery in the 5 years up to 2008. **41%** of BAAPS surgeons said they had seen no increase, while **43%** registered 'a little bit more' interest

According to a 2008 survey:

Nearly **1 in 10** under-35-year-olds would consider giving botox as a Christmas present to their spouse or partner

45% of 55–64-year-olds would be annoyed by such a gift

Half of 16–24-year-olds would feel insulted

91% of women would rather have a new kitchen than a facelift

Cigarettes and drugs

SMOKING: A DECLINING ADDICTION

1948: **65%** of men   **40%** of women

1974: **51%** of men   **41%** of women

2005: **25%** of men   **23%** of women

9% of children (11–15) smoke 1 or more cigarettes a week

In 2005 just over **two-thirds** of cigarette smokers said they wanted to give up

Manual workers and their families are almost **twice** as likely to smoke as those with a managerial or professional background

People living together are **twice** as likely to smoke as married couples

HARDCORE SMOKERS

The number of heavy smokers (20 or more cigarettes a day) has remained almost unchanged since 1998 (**10%** of men and **7%** of women)

The greatest proportion of smokers is to be found in the Northeast (**30%** in 2007)

16% of smokers have their first cigarette of the day within 5 minutes of waking up

Those most likely to smoke are 20–24-year-olds (around **1 in 3** in 2007)

DRUGS

The UK Drug Policy Commission has estimated that around **1 in 4** of 26–30-year-olds have tried Class A drugs (including heroin and cocaine) and that approaching half of all young people have used cannabis

Drug-related crime in England and Wales is estimated to cost **£13 billion** a year

The UK has the **highest** levels of addiction and the 2nd-highest rate of drug-related deaths (1,700 in 2004) in Europe

The economy

A STORY OF GENTLE DECLINE

In 1960 the UK was **second** only to the
USA in the league of world economies

By 2001 it was **fourth**, behind the USA, Japan and Germany

By 2008 it was **sixth**, behind the USA, China, Japan, India and Germany

WHO DOES WHAT?

British labour force, 2007:

Agriculture **1%**
Industry **18%**
Services **81%**

French labour force, 2005:

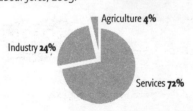

Agriculture **4%**
Industry **24%**
Services **72%**

Chinese labour force, 2006:

Services **32%**
Agriculture **43%**
Industry **25%**

DOWN ON THE FARM

In 1939 **1 in 22** employed people worked on a farm. By 2000 that figure had dropped to **1 in 77**

26% of the food that could be produced in the UK is now imported (an increase of **9%** over the past decade)

THE INDUSTRIAL SCENE

In 1981 **1 in 3** jobs held by men and **1 in 5** jobs held by women were in manufacturing

By 2001 that figure had dropped to **1 in 5** for men and **1 in 10** for women

In 1920 there were **1.25 million** miners at work in the UK. By 1998 that figure had dropped to **9,000** – a fall of **99%**

By the 1990s **30 times** more working days were being lost due to injury at work than to strike action

SERVICE WITH A SMILE

In 1981 financial and business services accounted for **1 in 10** jobs

By 2001 that figure had risen to **1 in 5** jobs

In 2003 **20%** of the UK's GDP was generated by London

The government valued the service economy at **£1 trillion** in 2008

Where does it all go?

THE RISING COST OF LIVING

If you took £1,000 from 2007 and travelled back to 1970 your money would buy you **£11,000** worth of goods and services. The figure for 1936 would be **£51,000**, and for 1750 **£160,000**

How we spend our money:

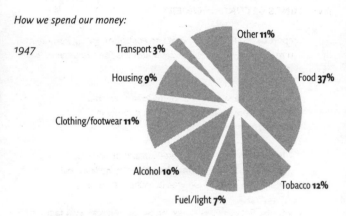

1947

Other **11%**

Transport **3%**

Food **37%**

Housing **9%**

Clothing/footwear **11%**

Alcohol **10%**

Tobacco **12%**

Fuel/light **7%**

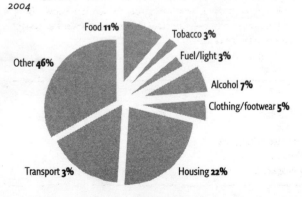

2004

Food **11%**

Tobacco **3%**

Fuel/light **3%**

Other **46%**

Alcohol **7%**

Clothing/footwear **5%**

Transport **3%**

Housing **22%**

THINGS WE CAN LIVE WITHOUT

Items in the 1947 'basket of goods' (used to calculate the
Retail Price Index) included:
mangles, corsets, candles, wireless licences

Items from 1947 which survived in the 2004 basket included:
hair cuts, postal charges, a woman's dress,
public transport fares, football admissions

ARE THINGS GETTING CHEAPER?

A 2008 report by the RAC found that the cost of motoring had fallen
by **18%** in real terms over the past 20 years, despite the price of fuel
rising by 210% in that time

> A survey at the same time found, however, that
> **60%** of people thought the biggest change in
> motoring over that period was higher costs

> In the same year it was estimated that prices in
> the Argos catalogue had decreased by **47%** in real
> terms since the chain was launched in 1973

According to the Retail Prices Index, prices overall rose by a factor of
10 between 1970 and 2004, with food prices rising more slowly (8
times) and houses much more quickly (36 times). In the same period
wages rose by a factor of **18**

Average cost of:

	1971	2007
A dozen large eggs	26p	£2.14
A pint of milk	5p	37p
Sliced white bread (800 grams)	10p	90p
Pint of beer	15p	£2.62
Pack of 20 cigarettes	27p	£5.02

Shop till you drop

THE RISE OF THE SUPERMARKET

Number of UK supermarkets:

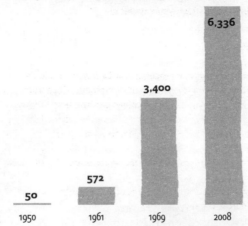

50	572	3,400	6,336
1950	1961	1969	2008

From the 1960s, chains were starting to emerge – Premier, Victor Value and Fine Fare had **330** stores between them. Three years later, Resale Price Maintenance (price-fixing arrangement between manufacturers) was abolished, and supermarkets started to take off

By 2007 there were only **4** chains left operating full-scale supermarkets of 40,000 square feet (3,700 square metres) or larger: Tesco, Asda, Sainsbury's and Morrisons

In the spring of that year, these **4** had a **75.63%** share of the UK grocery market

Harrods is the largest department store in the world, with over **1 million square feet** (92,900 square metres) of selling space. Its nearest UK rival, Selfridges, has **540,000 square feet** (50,200 square metres)

UK retailers hand out an estimated **13 billion** plastic bags each year (2006). Such bags take **1,000** years to decay

ON THE UP: TESCO

Jack Cohen began selling groceries from a stall in London's East End in 1919. In 1924 he bought a shipment of tea from T.E. Stockwell, and used those 3 initials plus the first 2 of his own surname to form his company's name. He opened his first store in Burnt Oak, Edgware, Middlesex in 1929

In 1994 Tesco became the first UK supermarket to issue a loyalty card

In 2006 Tesco became the world's **fourth** largest retailer (Wal-Mart is the biggest)

£1 in every **£3** spent on groceries in the UK is spent in Tesco

DOWN AND OUT: WOOLWORTHS

Woolworths opened their first British store in Liverpool in 1909

By the early 1930s Woolworths were opening a new branch every **18** days

Woolworths' best trading day ever was 5 December 2008 when **£27 million** was taken

It closed down a few weeks later

Money in the bank

45% of bank account customers have never switched banks.
60% have been with the same bank for 10 years or more

At the start of 2005, half the country's households had less
than **£1,500** in savings – and half of those had none at all

3 million adults do not have a bank
or building society current account

Average loan given out by a pawnbroker in 2005: **£120**

Number of loans redeemed within
the statutory 6 month period: **85%**

The UK has more credit cards in issue than any other European
country – and **13 million** more credit cards than there are people

THE HOLE IN THE WALL

The first UK cashpoints were opened by Barclays Bank
in 1967. Known as 'robot cashiers', they were operated
by single-use vouchers (issued with a pin number), each
of which dispensed a pack of ten **£1** notes

In 1975 plastic cards were introduced

Daily withdrawal limit (Barclays):

1975	**£50**
1981	**£100**
1988	**£200**
1996	**£300**

Number of cash machines in UK:

1993: **19,100**

2006: **60,428**

In the same period the number of separate withdrawals rose from **1.24 billion** to **2.75 billion**

Average value of a withdrawal in 2006: **£65.34**

BROKE BRITAIN

In April 2009 average household debt (excluding mortgages) stood at **£9,500** (**£59,765** including mortgages)

One person became bankrupt or entered an Individual Voluntary Arrangement every **3.5** minutes

One property was repossessed every **10** minutes

Between April 2008 and April 2009, the number of people missing a payment on a gas bill went up by a **third**

By March 2009 over **2 million** people were unemployed – the highest figure since Labour came to power in 1997

The rich

THE SUPER RICH

The Sunday Times Rich List 2009
lists Britain's 1,000 richest people

Amount needed to be on the list: **£80 million**

Less than half of the top 20 were actually born in Britain;
these include:

Duke of Westminster:	**£6.5 billion**
Sir Philip Green:	**£3.83 billion**
Earl Cadogan:	**£2 billion**
Sir Ken Morrison:	**£1.61 billion**

You have to go down to number **44**
before you reach a non-billionaire

Queen Elizabeth II ranks **214th** (£270 million)

Even the rich, though, have been affected by the
recession. By early 2009 there were **23%** fewer
billionaires in the world than there had been a year
before, and the top 1,000 on *The Sunday Times* list were
£155 billion poorer than they had been a year before

FOR THE BILLIONAIRE WITH EVERYTHING

£26,388 for a night in the Royal Presidential Suite,
President Wilson Hotel, Geneva (2007)

£31,402 for a bottle of Château d'Yquem Sauternes, 1787 (2008)

£810,345 for a Bugatti Veyron (2005)

THE MERELY RICH

Number of British millionaires:

1809: 8
1900: 100
1979: 1,800
2006: 376,000

According to EU statistics for 2006 the UK
has a bigger gap between the best paid and
worst paid than the EU average (behind
Germany and France, for example). Sweden is
the most equal nation; Latvia is the least

By 2005 there were more female millionaires than male in the
18–44 age range. Scotland has more female millionaires than male

In 2000, if your surname was Patel you were **7 times**
more likely to be a multi-millionaire than if it was Smith

By 2007 there were nearly **500,000** people in the UK worth
£500,000 or more (not including their primary property)

Education

THE NATION'S SCHOOLS

State education:
9.7 million pupils
at 33,666 schools
in the UK in 2007–8

Private education:
600,000 pupils.
Average annual school
fees in 2008: £10,239

According to the Sutton Trust in 2007, more than **half** of the leading figures in UK politics, medicine, law, business and journalism were privately educated

There are now 3 times as many 3- and 4-year-old children in school (**64%**) as there were in 1970–1

More than twice as many children from 'professional' homes gained 5 A* to C grades at GCSE level in 2002 as those with parents in 'routine' occupations

Nearly **63,000** children played truant every day in 2008 – the highest rate since records began in 1997

WHAT GETS STUDIED

In 2008 the 10 most popular GCSE subjects were:

1. Maths
2. English
3. English Literature
4. Science
5. Additional Science
6. Design and Technology
7. History
8. Art
9. Geography
10. French

The numbers studying French have declined markedly over the past few years. Spanish, however, has increased in popularity

GETTING A DEGREE

In 2006–7 there were **3.6 million** students in further education in the UK – more than twice the number in 1970–1

In 2006–7 the most popular subjects for men to study were:

1. Business and administrative studies
2. Engineering and technology
3. Computer science

In 2006–7 the most popular subjects for women to study were:

1. Medicine
2. Education
3. Business and administrative studies

82% of barristers were Oxbridge educated

Books and newspapers

A GOOD READ

The most popular places to read around the house are:

1 In bed (**65%**)
2 In the bath (**25%**)
3 On the loo (**10%**)

More men than women read books on the loo

10 best-selling books in 2008:

1 *The Tales of Beedle the Bard* J.K. Rowling **856,268**
2 *Guinness World Records 2009* **691,103**
3 *At My Mother's Knee ... and Other Low Joints* Paul O'Grady **664,474**
4 *No Time for Goodbye* Linwood Barclay **643,225**
5 *A Thousand Splendid Suns* Khaled Hosseini **610,181**
6 *Dear Fatty* Dawn French **589,729**
7 *Jamie's Ministry of Food* Jamie Oliver **543,283**
8 *Delia's How to Cheat at Cooking* Delia Smith **525,881**
9 *That's Another Story: The Autobiography* Julie Walters **476,897**
10 *Parky: My Autobiography* Michael Parkinson **445,702**

An average
£150 million
worth of books
a year are stolen
each year from
UK libraries

I NEVER MANAGED TO FINISH IT

In a Teletext poll in 2007 the novels readers most commonly confessed that they couldn't finish were:

1 *Vernon God Little* D.B.C. Pierre (**35%**)
2 *Harry Potter and the Goblet of Fire* J.K. Rowling (**32%**)
3 *Ulysses* James Joyce (**28%**)

Just over **1 in 3** people never read books

READ ALL ABOUT IT

In 2008 the *Sun* was read by just over **1 in 6** adults

The top-selling broadsheet, the *Daily Telegraph*, was read by **1 in 25**

The *Sun*'s highest ever daily sales came on 18 November 1995, when over **4.8 million** copies were sold

In 1977–8 nearly **three-quarters** of all adults read a national daily newspaper

By 2007–8 only **half** did

Mind your language

Top 5 languages spoken in the UK:

	Language	Approximate number of speakers
1	English	**58.2 million**
2	Welsh	**582,000**
3	Eastern Punjabi	**471,000**
4=	Bengali	**400,000**
4=	Urdu	**400,000**

Other languages spoken in the UK include:

Scottish Gaelic (**58,652** speakers in the 2001 census)
Manx (perhaps **1,689** speakers)
Cornwall (around **600** speakers)
Gaelic in Northern Ireland (**95,000** speakers)

EVERYDAY WORDS

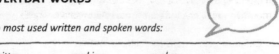

10 most used written and spoken words:

written	ranking	spoken
the	1	be
of	2	the
and	3	I
a	4	you
in	5	and
to	6	it
is	7	have
was	8	a
it	9	not
for	10	do

OLDEST WORDS

Researchers at Reading University claim that among the oldest words in the English language – dating back many thousands of years – are:

I
we
two
three

RUDE WORDS

A 2009 *Panorama* poll suggested that **55%** of us think there is too much swearing on radio and television

> The BBC's own guidelines list **3** swearwords whose use has to be specifically cleared before they can be broadcast

However, we are not that virtuous ourselves. The average Briton utters **14** expletives a day, men being marginally more foul-mouthed (**90%** swearing every day) than women (**83%**)

> Different generations take different views. **21%** of those aged 50–60 think bad language is a problem, but only **6%** of 18-30-year-olds agree

Dumb Britain

COULD DO BETTER

Surveys in 2007 and 2008 revealed that:

> **1 in 3** primary school pupils
> thought that Winston Churchill
> was the first man to walk on the moon

> **25%** of adults didn't believe Churchill existed at all

2 in 5 primary school pupils thought that there is
no planet Mars, only a chocolate bar of that name

> **10%** of 8-year-olds didn't know that pork chops come from pigs

An article in the Times Higher Education *magazine in 2008 bewailed
university students' inability to spell, and suggested that the 10 common
words most frequently misspelt were:*

Arguement

Febuary

Wensday

Ignor

Occured

Opertunity

Queue

Speach

Thier

Twelth

Truely

6.8 million adults in the UK have maths skills below that expected of an 11-year-old

> In England, **16%** of adults have 'low skills' (the level expected of an 11-year-old or below); in Wales, the figure is **25%**, in Scotland **23%** and in Northern Ireland **24%**

Fewer than **1 in 5** parents feel confident about helping children aged 11 and over with their homework

$$24 \div 4 =$$
$$5 \times 6 =$$
$$15 - 3 =$$
$$3 \times 7 =$$

COULD DO WORSE

> A 2006 survey of national IQs placed Britain **8th** in Europe, with an average IQ of **100**. This is lower than Germany and the Netherlands (**107**), but ahead of Spain (**98**), France (**94**) and Turkey (**90**)

In Victorian times, only **50%** of adults could read at all

The figure is now closer to **97%** in England

Our leaders

WHO ARE THEY?

Profession: Among MPs returned to Parliament at the 2001 general election, the most common occupations across the 3 major parties were teacher (**117**) and company executive (**77**)

The proportion of female to male MPs: (▓ men ▓ women)

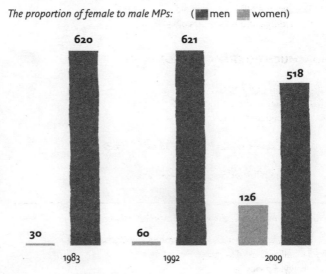

620 **621** **518**

126

30 60

1983 1992 2009

Ethnic origins: **15** MPs elected in 2005 were from ethnic minorities

WHERE WERE THEY EDUCATED?

Overall, a third of MPs went to fee-paying schools.
6 out of 10 Conservatives were privately educated,
while just under **2 out of 10** Labour MPs were

36% of Tony Blair's Cabinet in 2000
had been to Oxford or Cambridge

Back in 1964 **10 out of 23** of Alec Douglas-Home's
Cabinet had been educated at Eton, and only 3 had
not been to public school

HOW OLD ARE THEY?

The average MP is **51** years old;
the average lord is **68** years old

HOW MUCH DO THEY GET PAID?

MP: **£64,766** (April 2009).
This is similar to the average salary
of aircraft pilots and engineers

Cabinet minister: **£141,866** (April 2008)

Prime Minister: **£194,250** (April 2008)

In addition, MPs can claim various expenses, including:

Cost of staying away from main home: **£23,083** (2007/8)
Staffing allowance: **£90,505**
Stationery: **£7,000**

In 2003–4 government ministers spent
nearly **£11.5 million** on wining and dining

Electing our leaders ✗

GETTING THE VOTE: A BRIEF HISTORY

1832 Reform Act: extends the vote to **1 in 7** adult males
1884: vote extended to around **6 in 10** of all men
1918: men over **21** and women over **30** can vote
1928: age restriction for women dropped to **21**
1969: all men and women over **18** can vote

HOW MANY VOTE?

*Turnouts at Westminster General Elections
(percentage of the electorate voting):*

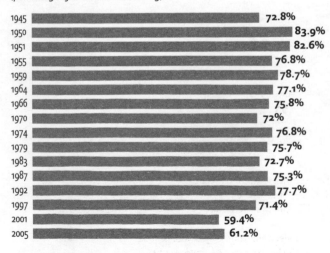

Year	Turnout
1945	72.8%
1950	83.9%
1951	82.6%
1955	76.8%
1959	78.7%
1964	77.1%
1966	75.8%
1970	72%
1974	76.8%
1979	75.7%
1983	72.7%
1987	75.3%
1992	77.7%
1997	71.4%
2001	59.4%
2005	61.2%

*1974 figure is an average of the February election
(78.8%) and the October election (72.8%)

At the 2005 election, Labour won only **36%** of the vote, the lowest support for a government since the Great Reform Act of 1832

Not a single MP was elected by half of the electorate in any constituency

Only **2** MPs won more than **40%** of the vote

In 1999 the European election hit an all-time low of a **24%** turnout

FIRST PAST THE POST

The 'first past the post' system that operates in the UK can produce some strange results. For instance, at the 1951 General Election:

Votes cast:

Conservative: **12,660,061**
Labour: **13,948,883**

But the seats won were:

Conservative: **302**
Labour: **295**

With the help of the National Liberals (**19** seats) the Conservatives achieved a majority of **17**

Despite the tumultuous scenes in Downing Street on 2 May 1997, Tony Blair had just gained fewer votes (**13,518,167**) than John Major had in winning the election 5 years previously (**14,093,007**)

Indeed the Tories' 1992 vote is still the largest received by any party in any UK General Election ever

The voters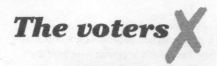

WHO IS WORKING CLASS?

According to one survey in 2007 **57%** of us regard ourselves as working class

However, only **31%** of the population of working age are in occupations traditionally regarded as 'working class' (e.g. manual and unskilled)

The areas of the UK that have the highest proportion of people in 'routine occupations' and 'semi-routine occupations' are the Northeast, Yorkshire and the West Midlands

In a 2006 survey, **500,000** people who earned more than **£100,000** a year said they regarded themselves as working class

WHO IS MIDDLE CLASS?

More people now regard themselves as middle class than did in the 1960s: roughly **1 in 3** now as opposed to **1 in 4** then

Middle-class people live in properties worth on average **70%** more than those owned by those who regard themselves as working class

In a 2006 survey, people who described themselves as working class were more likely to say that income determined social class, while those who described themselves as middle class tended to cite education, property and where you live

London and the Southeast have the highest proportions of people in higher managerial and professional occupations (**14.5%** of the working population, compared with **6.6%** in Northern Ireland, **7.9%** in the Northeast, **8.2%** in Wales and **9.5%** in Scotland)

Proportion of builders who regard themselves as middle class: **36%**

Proportion of bank managers who regard themselves as working class: **29%**

Proportion of working- and middle-class people who own their own home:

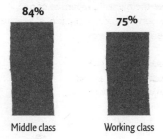

84%	75%
Middle class	Working class

WHAT HAPPENED TO THE UPPER CLASS?

In 2005 **69%** of the land in the UK was owned by **0.6%** of the population – mostly families who had held it since Victorian times

103 people in Scotland owned **30%** of the land

Servants of the people

THE RELENTLESS RISE OF THE RULING CLASS

1900: the British government contained
60 ministers, **19** of whom were in the Cabinet

1940: there were **74** ministers

2007: Gordon Brown's first government contained
137 posts (some ministers occupied more than one)

2008: the government included such posts as:

Secretary of State for Communities
Minister of State for Culture, Creative Industries and Tourism
Minister for the North-West
Minister for the Third Sector
Parliamentary Under-Secretary of State for Climate Change,
  Biodiversity and Waste
Parliamentary Under-Secretary of State for Skills

The Belgian constitution limits the number
of ministers in their government to **15**

THE ART OF RED TAPE

*Number of printed pages required to print legislation
that has been passed:*

1911: Acts of Parliament **430**

   Statutory Instruments (the main form in which
   delegated or secondary legislation is made) **330**

2003: Acts of Parliament **4,073**

   Statutory Instruments **8,942**

Number of words in the 10 Commandments: **313**

Number of words in the Salmon and Freshwater Fisheries
(Consolidation) (Scotland) Act 2003: **21,000**

THE BUREAUCRATIC JUNGLE

By 2001, the number of people in the British Civil Service
was the same as the population of Sheffield (**513,000**)

Just under **53%** of the Civil Service
in 2007 were women

Just over **30%** of Senior Civil Servants
in 2007 were women

75% of young French people say they
would like to become civil servants

Paying for it all

INCOME TAX

Income tax accounts for **29%** of government revenue
(approximately **£155 billion** in 2008-9). National Insurance
provides the next biggest chunk (**19%** or **£104.6 billion**)

> In 1974 the top rate of income tax increased to its highest since
> the Second World War: **83%** on incomes over **£20,000** a year.
> It is now **50%** on earnings over £150,000 a year

VAT

Value Added Tax, which raised nearly **£84 billion** in 2008-9,
is applied to purchases – but not all purchases. Some items are
exempt – which can give lawyers a field (and indeed pay) day

> In 2008 Marks and Spencer won a 12-year dispute with the
> Treasury, when the European Court of Justice agreed with them
> that their teacakes were indeed cakes (zero-rated) and not biscuits
> (which are subject to VAT). Similarly, McVities had to go to court to
> prove that Jaffa Cakes are indeed cakes

> > In 2008 the UK High Court ruled that Pringles are
> > not crisps – the snack only has a **42%** potato content –
> > and therefore are free from VAT

OTHER CLEVER WAYS OF RAISING MONEY

Recent revenue-raising schemes have included:

Landfill tax (introduced in 1996): raised **£1.1 billion** in 2008/9

Climate change levy (introduced in 2001): raised **£0.7 billion** in 2008/9

TAX DODGERS

Fraudulent welfare claims and claim errors cost the country around **£1 billion** a year. In 2003, **11,000** individuals were prosecuted

Fraudulent tax returns and tax evasion cost the country **£2–3 billion** a year. In 2003, **60** individuals were prosecuted

WHAT DOES IT ALL GO ON?

Major items of projected central government expenditure 2007/8:

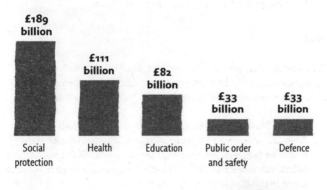

| £189 billion | £111 billion | £82 billion | £33 billion | £33 billion |
| Social protection | Health | Education | Public order and safety | Defence |

What do we believe?

IN GOD AND GHOSTS WE TRUST

In the 2001 census **71.6%** of British people described themselves as Christian, but only **38%** of us believe in God

More of us believe in ghosts than in God – some **42%**

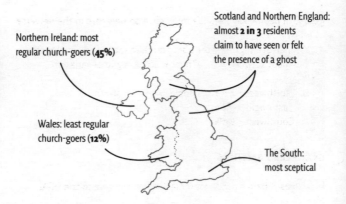

Scotland and Northern England: almost **2 in 3** residents claim to have seen or felt the presence of a ghost

Northern Ireland: most regular church-goers (**45%**)

Wales: least regular church-goers (**12%**)

The South: most sceptical

A 2008 survey of Fellows of the Royal Society found that **3.3%** of them believed in God

OLD NICK

32% of Britons believe in the Devil
28% believe in hell
1,500 registered themselves as Satanists on the 2001 census

THE FUNDAMENTAL QUESTION

In a 2006 survey on what best described people's view of the 'origin and development of life', responses were as follows:

Evolution: **48%**
Creationism: **22%**
Intelligent design: **17%**
Don't know: **13%**

ENCOUNTERS OF THE THIRD KIND

50.2% of people say alien life must exist somewhere in the universe

Women are slightly more sceptical than men, and pensioners the most sceptical of all. There is some regional variation

Northwest – **43%** of people believe in aliens
East Anglia – **58%**
Southwest – **65%**

GOD BLESS AMERICA

How does Britain's godliness (or lack of it) compare to the USA?

A third of the American population (**100 million** people) are Evangelical Protestants by affiliation

Even **62.9%** of those Americans not affiliated with a religious tradition believe in God or some higher power

71.5% of Americans pray at least once a week, while **49.2%** attend church at least once a month

Who believes what?

CHRISTIANITY

1 in 4.5 of us is, nominally at least, an Anglican. Only **1 in 36** of us, however, attends church on a regular basis

1 in 10 of us is a Roman Catholic (in Northern Ireland, Roman Catholics account for **43.8%** of the population)

1 in 185 of us is a Methodist

Number of churches:

1961: **55,000**
2005: **47,600**
2020 (estimate): **43,000**

Churches are now closing faster than new mosques are opening

ISLAM

Britain's first mosque was recorded in 1860, at 2 Glyn Rhondda Street in Cardiff

By 1961 there were **7** mosques, and, by 1985, **338**

Today there are **1,689** mosques in the UK, attended by **1 million** regular worshippers. The total number of Muslims in the UK is around **1.8 million**

JUDAISM

Jews were expelled from England in 1290 and readmitted by Cromwell in 1655. Large-scale immigration occurred in late-Victorian times

The Jewish population of Britain fell from **340,000** in 1990 to **270,000** in 2006. A mid-1990s report found that nearly **1 in 2** were marrying non-Jews. Sunderland's synagogue closed in 2006 after the number of attendants fell from a high of **1,000** to **30**

AND OTHERS

According to the 2001 census there are **31,000** pagans, **7,000** Wicca and **5,000** Rastafarians

In the same census, **390,000** people wrote 'Jedi' as their religion (in response to a campaign) – if it had been listed it would have come fourth, below Christianity, Islam and Hinduism, but above Sikhism and Judaism

A 2005 Mori poll revealed that while just over **1 in 10** of those aged 65 said that they had no religious beliefs, among those aged 18–34 the proportion was **1 in 3**

How much crime is there? 〣〣〣〣 ||||

Crimes recorded by the police (England and Wales):

1952 **513,559**

2000–1 **over 5 million**

Violent crimes:

1952 **4,100**

2000–1 **55,000**

Proportion of all thefts that involve vehicles:

1952 **13%**

2000–1 **46%**

Prison population:

1952 **51,803**

2000–1 **69,850**

Number of police officers:

1952 **65,742**

2000–1 **127,231**

Crime figures for Scotland and Northern Ireland are recorded differently. A UN survey in 2005, however, put Scotland ahead of England, Wales and Northern Ireland for levels of violent crime, claiming that the number of incidents had doubled in 10 years and that **2,000** Scots were now being attacked each week (**10 times** the official police figures)

THE BAD BOYS OF EUROPE

The 2007 European Crime and Safety Survey found that the UK came **second** (behind the Republic of Ireland) in the European league of crime

Other 'crime hotspots' (countries with crime rates higher than average) were Estonia, the Netherlands, Belgium and Denmark

Rates of particular crimes in the UK:

Highest levels of assaults (with threats, not force) in the EU (**5%** of the population were victims at some point in 2004)

The most burgled country in the EU (**3%**) – this despite having the 2nd-highest rate of burglar alarms (after Ireland)

A higher than average level of hate crimes (**3%**)

High risk of theft from cars (**5%**; EU average **3.5%**)

High risk of personal theft (**5.8%**; EU average **3.5%**)

Pickpocketing and personal theft: the UK, Ireland and Estonia were above the EU average

One area of crime in which the UK ranked low was attempted bribery. The country where corruption was deemed most likely was Greece

Is crime getting worse?

A rising trend in reported crime began in 1954 and peaked in 1995 at **19 million** crimes

> Since then, the level has fallen – to **10.9 million** in 2005–6

Recorded crime, England and Wales:

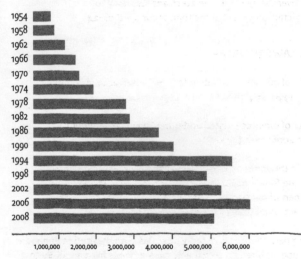

The Northern Ireland Crime Survey of 2005 suggested that only **60%** of crime committed in Northern Ireland was actually reported to police. For England and Wales the rate was **53%** and for Scotland **50%**

TOO SCARED TO GO OUT?

A European Commission report in 2004 suggested that Britons were living in greater fear of crime than any other European nation. It suggested that this was why **90%** of Britons supported the use of high-street CCTV, compared with only **48%** of Germans and **24%** of Austrians

According to Age Concern in 2003, **half** of all those aged over **75** were too fearful of being mugged or verbally abused to leave their house after dark

People over the age of **60** are **20 times** less likely to be the victims of violent crime than those aged **16–24**

MORE LAWS TO BREAK?

Number of offences created under the Conservative government, 1988 to 1996: **494**

Number of offences created under the Labour government, 1997 to 2006: over **3,000**

In this latter period the Department for the Environment and Rural Affairs alone came up with **640**, including (as part of the Natural Environment and Rural Communities Act 2006) making it illegal to sell a grey squirrel

Devising new offences is nothing new. Between about 1680 and 1722 the number of offences punishable by death rose from about **80** to over **350**, including:

'being in the company of Gypsies for one month'

'strong evidence of malice in a child aged **7–14** years of age'

The nature of the crime

Commonest crimes 2007/8:

England and Wales
1 Theft and handling stolen goods
2 Criminal damage
3 Violence against the person

Scotland
1 Theft and handling stolen goods
2 Criminal damage
3 Drugs offences

Northern Ireland
1 Criminal damage
2 Violence against the person
3 Theft and handling stolen goods

GETTING AWAY WITH MURDER

In England and Wales in the 1890s there was an average of **350** murders a year (approximately 1 murder per 100,000 of population) The level fell from 1900 onwards, reaching **0.6** murders per 100,000 in the 1960s, then doubled by the 1980s, reaching **1.45** murders per 100,000 in 1995. Since then it has fallen back to **1.37** in 2008

In 2005, Glasgow was the Murder Capital of Europe, with **70** killings (mostly related to the drug trade)

You are more than **4 times** more likely to be murdered in Colombia than in England and Wales

MURDER WEAPONS

The 5 most common murder weapons and methods in England and Wales are:

1 Sharp instrument
2 Hitting and kicking
3 Unknown
4 Blunt instrument
5 Strangulation

BREAKING AND ENTERING

Burglary rates in England and Wales fell to **733,000** in 2005–6, down **59%** from the peak of **1.77 million** in 1995

6% of burglars are women

Burglars gain access through unlocked doors and windows in **1 in 5** cases

DID YOU PAY FOR THAT?

On average a shoplifting offence takes place every 90 seconds and accounts for **64%** of all retail crime losses (**16%** = burglary, **8%** = robberies, **8%** = employee theft). England and Wales have the highest rate in Europe

Children are among the worst offenders, particularly those aged 13–15; **48%** come from well-to-do backgrounds

Most popular items stolen: batteries, razor blades, vodka, condoms, smoked salmon, designer clothes, mascara and lingerie

Criminal behaviour

YOUNG OFFENDERS

In the early 1890s, **20%** of people convicted
were under **16** and another **20%** under **21**

The age of criminal responsibility
was lowered from **14** to **10** in 1997

In 2006–7, **295,000** offences were committed
by those aged between **10** and **17**

59,000 of those were committed by girls –
up from **12,000** in 2003–4

Between June 2000 and 31 December 2006 **30** boys aged **10**
were issued with ASBOs (Anti-Social Behaviour Orders). The most
common age for someone under **18** to receive an ASBO is **16**

But young people are also more likely to be the victims
of crime. In 2006 over a quarter of those aged under **26**
were victims at some point in the previous 12 months

 ## TOOLS OF THE TRADE

In 2004–5 firearms were used in **1 in every 250** crimes

50% of the firearms involved were air weapons

The British Crime Survey suggested that there were **169,000**
violent incidents involving knives in 2005–6 – half the 1995 level

More than **half** the knives seized by police in
Scotland in 2008 were in the Glasgow area

 **FUELLED UP**

A 1999 survey across **6** cities in England found that a significant proportion of those arrested tested positive for alcohol

---

Percentage of those arrested in 1999 survey who tested positive for alcohol:

assault **32%**
robbery **75%**
criminal damage **29%**
breach of the peace **61%**
theft of/taking vehicle **30%**

40% of the victims of violent crime say that their assailant was under the influence of drink

FEAR OF CRIME

Although crime is generally falling, fear of crime is increasing. In 2007–8, **65%** of people thought that there was more crime than the previous year

*Risk of being a victim of violent crime, 2007–8
(according to the British Crime Survey):*

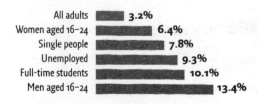

All adults	3.2%
Women aged 16–24	6.4%
Single people	7.8%
Unemployed	9.3%
Full-time students	10.1%
Men aged 16–24	13.4%

Centres of crime

England and Wales 2006:

Leeds: 2nd most dangerous town/city to live (107.2 crimes per 1,000 residents)

Nottingham: most dangerous town/city to live (115.5 crimes per 1,000 residents); worst for murder and vehicle crime

Bradford: worst for gun crime

Manchester: worst for robbery

Colchester: 3rd safest town/city to live (33.9 crimes per 1,000 residents)

Stockport: 3rd most dangerous town/city to live (100.42 crimes per 1,000 residents); worst for burglary

Leicester: worst for assault

Portsmouth: worst for rape

Southend: safest town/city to live (30 crimes per 1,000 residents)

Poole: 2nd safest town/city to live (32.7 crimes per 1,000 residents)

CAPITAL CRIMES

London in 2006 was the **29th** most dangerous town/city in England and Wales

If individual boroughs had been ranked separately, Kingston upon Thames, Sutton and Richmond would have been near the bottom of the league table

Westminster would have been the **7th** most dangerous in the country, Islington **10th** and Hackney **11th**

OVER THE BORDER

Scottish cities with the highest levels of crime, 2003:

Glasgow (**136** crimes per 1,000 residents)
Aberdeen (**118** crimes per 1,000 residents)
Dundee (**115** crimes per 1,000 residents)

ACROSS THE SEA

The Northern Ireland Crime Survey for 2005 found that there was a lower risk of being a victim of crime in Northern Ireland (**1 in 5.8**) than in England and Wales (**1 in 4.2**)

Detection

SMILE, YOU'RE ON CAMERA

The UK has an estimated **5 million** CCTV cameras, **1 for every 12** citizens – the greatest camera-incidence of any country in the world

> A representative of a UK police force said in 2007 that **80%** of the CCTV images he was asked to examine were 'totally useless' as potential evidence

Only an estimated **3%** of London's street robberies in 2008 were solved using CCTV footage

> When people were given a still picture of somebody and asked to pick them out of a series of CCTV stills – taken in identical lighting conditions, and with the subject displaying a similar facial expression – in **30%** of cases they picked the wrong person or could not find them at all

> In 2007 staff at an Aldershot pub asked a customer to remove her hat so she could be seen by security cameras. The customer was an 87-year-old and the hat had been hand-crocheted

'ALLO, 'ALLO, 'ALLO ...

In 2007–8, Home Office figures for the 43 police forces in England and Wales showed that in a typical 12-hour shift, officers spent **1 hour and 39 minutes** actually on the beat

YOU'RE NICKED

Police clear-up rates:

1952 **47%**

2000–1 **24%**

In 2006–7 the detection rate for all crimes in England and Wales was **27%**. Almost all of these (1.4 million offences) were 'sanction detections' – those which resulted in someone being charged, cautioned, given a warning or some form of judicial penalty

A further **80,000** offences were non-sanction detections – those where the police knew who was responsible but no further judicial action was taken (e.g. when a witness could not give evidence, or the Crown Prosecution Service dropped the case)

Best and worst forces for sanction detections, England and Wales, 2006–7:

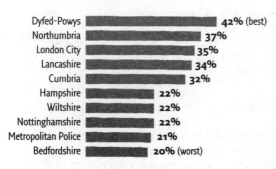

Dyfed-Powys		**42%** (best)
Northumbria		**37%**
London City		**35%**
Lancashire		**34%**
Cumbria		**32%**
Hampshire		**22%**
Wiltshire		**22%**
Nottinghamshire		**22%**
Metropolitan Police		**21%**
Bedfordshire		**20%** (worst)

78% of murders committed in London in 2003–4 were solved

Just over **1,000** serving police officers have criminal records

The sentence of the court

*Some of the crimes for which the law provides
a maximum sentence:*

Life imprisonment:

Hijacking
Casting stone, etc, upon a railway carriage, with intent
  to endanger the safety of any person therein
Impeding a person endeavouring to save himself from shipwreck
Using chloroform to commit an indictable offence

---

14 years:

Blackmail
Fraudulently printing, mutilating or re-issuing stamps

---

10 years:

Harbouring escaped prisoner
Making counterfeit coin or note intending that he or another
  shall pass it as genuine
Riot

---

7 years:

Child abduction
Bigamy
Placing or dispatching articles to cause a bomb hoax
Insider dealing
Perjury

---

5 years:

Assault occasioning actual bodily harm
Shortening a shotgun
Abstracting of electricity

3 years:

Taking, distributing, showing, possessing with a view to distributing
   or showing, advertising, etc an indecent photograph of a child
Agricultural charge fraud

2 years:

Falsely describing or presenting food
Dangerous driving
Unqualified person acting as a solicitor
Intercourse with an animal

6 months:

Assaulting a police officer
Making obscene or malicious telephone calls
Selling or letting for hire a crossbow to a person under 17
Cruelty to animals
Sexual offences in a public lavatory

ꤜꤜꤜꤜꤜꤜꤜꤜꤜꤜꤜꤜꤜꤜꤜꤜꤜꤜꤜꤜ

Extreme penalties

PRISON

England and Wales

Prisons:	**139**
Prisoners (2006):	**79,861**
Prisoners per 100,000 of population:	**148**

Scotland

Prisons:	**15**
Prisoners (2006:)	**7,131**
Prisoners per 100,000 of population:	**139**

Northern Ireland

Prisons:	**3**
Prisoners (2006):	**1,466**
Prisoners per 100,000 of population:	**81**

Incarceration rates (per 100,000 population), 2006:

USA (highest in world) **738**

Russia (2nd highest) **611**

St Kitts and Nevis (3rd highest) **547**

Luxembourg (highest in Western Europe) **167**

England and Wales (2nd highest in Western Europe) **148**

Iceland has the lowest level of incarceration in Europe, and the Faroe Islands have the lowest level in the world (an average of **7** prisoners at any one time)

Approximately **two-thirds** of prisoners in the UK are reconvicted within **2** years of release

THERE ARE WORSE THINGS THAN BEING LOCKED UP

Last beheading in England **1747**
Last burning at stake **1789**
Last public hanging **1868**
Last woman hanged **1955**
Last man hanged **1964**

The death penalty technically still survived, even after the abolition of the death penalty in 1965, for the following crimes:

Causing a fire or explosion in a naval dockyard, ship, magazine or warehouse (until **1971**)

Espionage (until **1981**)

Treason (until **1998**)

Piracy with violence (until **1998**)

Certain crimes under the jurisdiction of the armed forces, such as mutiny (until **1998**)

The armed forces

HOW MANY FIGHT?

Largest military powers in the world (numbers of troops):

1	China	**2,255,000**
2	USA	**1,380,000**
3	India	**1,325,000**
4	Russia	**1,245,000**
5	N.Korea	**1,106,000**
6	S.Korea	**687,000**
7	Pakistan	**610,000**
8	Iran	**545,000**
9	Turkey	**514,000**
10	Vietnam	**484,000**
28	UK	**195,000**

The Royal Navy is the **2nd** largest navy in the world (in terms of gross tonnage). In 2006, it had **90** commissioned ships, and a personnel of **35,470**

The US Navy, the largest in the world, is bigger than the next **17** biggest navies combined

Britain's budget for government quangos is **5 times** its budget for defence. In 2008 the Conservatives claimed that defence spending, as a proportion of the nation's GDP, was at its lowest rate since 1930

THE HARDWARE

2008 National Audit Office estimates for the cost of major projects:

Future Lynx (small helicopter):	**£1.9 billion**
Astute Class Submarine:	**£3.8 billion**
Beyond Visual Range Air-to-Air Missile (Meteor):	**£1.2 billion**

Possible cost of replacing Trident nuclear missile system, according to some 2006 reports: **£76 billion**

THE NUCLEAR CLUB

Number of strategic nuclear warheads held by nuclear powers:

Russia	**2,800**
USA	**2,200**
France	**300**
China	**180**
UK	**160**
Israel	**80**
Pakistan	**60**
India	**60**

It has been estimated that **50** of today's nuclear weapons could kill **200 million** people (roughly the population of the UK, France and Germany combined)

Armed conflict

*Britain's deadliest conflicts of the 20th century
(number of military deaths):*

First World War
(1914–18)
885,138

Second World War
(1939–45)
382,600

Second Boer War (1899–1902)	**22,000**
Third Anglo-Afghan war (1919)	**1,136**
Korean War (1950–3)	**1,109**
Russian Civil War (1918–20)	**1,073**

2,978 people were killed by the troubles in Northern Ireland
between 1969–99, of whom **1,123** were soldiers

258 British soldiers were killed during the 1982
Falklands War. The number of veterans of that war
who have since committed suicide is at least **264**

British military losses in Afghanistan from
the invasion of 2001–mid-July 2009: **184**

British military losses in Iraq from March 2003–April 2009: **179**

THE BIGGER PICTURE

Percentage of the world's population killed in major conflicts:

Napoleonic Wars:	**0.2%**
First World War:	**0.5%**
Second World War:	**2.4%**

1,000 British civilians were killed during the First World War

228,000 civilians then died during the flu pandemic of 1918–19

671,000 civilians were killed during the Second World War

TERRORIST TARGETS

Major losses of life in terrorist attacks and campaigns in the UK:

1972 Northern Ireland: **479** (worst year of the Troubles)
1974 England: **38** (IRA campaign);
      Northern Ireland: **204**
      (the Troubles)
1982 England: **11** (IRA campaign);
      Northern Ireland **110** (the Troubles)
1988 Scotland: **270** (bombing of Pan Am flight 103 at Lockerbie);
      Northern Ireland **104** (the Troubles)
1998 Northern Ireland: **55**
      (including **29** killed in the Omagh bombing)
2005 England: **56** (suicide bombings in London)

Royalty

IF YOU ONLY KNOW ONE THING ...

HENRY VIII (1491–1547)

The **6 foot 2 inch** (1.9 metre) monarch weighed nearly **30 stone** (190 kilograms). It took **16** Yeomen of the Guard to carry his coffin

CHARLES I (1600–49)

Didn't speak until he was **5**, didn't walk until he was **7**, and grew to only **4 foot 7 inches** (1.4 metres)

QUEEN ANNE (1665–1714)

Had **17** children in 16 years, all of whom died young or were stillborn. Longest surviving was William, Duke of Gloucester, who died in 1700 at the age of 11

GEORGE 1 (1660–1727)

Spent approximately **one-fifth** of his reign in Germany, the country of his birth

GEORGE III (1738–1820)

Collected **67,000** books

GEORGE IV (1762–1830)

Had a **50-inch** (127-centimetre) waist

WILLIAM IV (1765–1837)

Had **10** illegitimate children (5 of each gender) with the actress Dorothea Bland – but no legitimate children, so was succeeded by his niece Victoria

VICTORIA (1819–1901)

At her birth, Victoria was **5th** in line to the throne

EDWARD VII (1841–1910)

Among the items served at his 14-course coronation banquet were **2,500** plump quails, **300** legs of mutton and **80** chickens. One of the dessert dishes, *Caisses de fraises Miramare* – a strawberry dish – took **3** days to make

GEORGE V (1865–1936)

On 18 December 1913 he shot over **1,000** pheasants in **6** hours, later admitting that 'we went a little too far'

EDWARD VIII (1894–1972)

Had **7** Christian names (Edward Albert Christian George Andrew Patrick David), the last **4** being the patron saints of England, Scotland, Ireland and Wales

GEORGE VI (1895–1952)

Bagged **1,055** woodcock in the course of his hunting career

The queen

Queen Elizabeth II is the **40th** sovereign
since William the Conqueror

She and her husband are second cousins once
removed through King Christian IX of Denmark,
and third cousins through Queen Victoria

They received over **2,500** wedding gifts

The naval ratings who lined the route of her coronation were ordered
to abstain from alcohol and sexual intercourse for the preceding **48**
hours, in order to preserve the purity of the occasion

She has owned over **30 corgis** during her reign, most
of them being direct descendants of the first, Susan

During her Silver Jubilee (the summer of 1977), she performed
a tour of the UK and Commonwealth, travelling an estimated
56,000 miles (90,000 kilometres)

In London, **4,000** street parties were reported

By the time of her Golden Jubilee (June 2002), she had:

Conferred **380,630** honours and awards at **459** investitures

Granted Royal Assent to **3,135** Acts of Parliament

Performed **251** official overseas visits to **128** countries

Sat for **120** official portraits

Sent almost **100,000** telegrams to centenarians

Attended **31** Royal Variety performances

Hosted **88** state banquets

Launched **17** ships

Sent **37,500** Christmas cards

Distributed **75,000** Christmas puddings
to the Royal Household

Distributed Maundy money to over **5,000** people

She was also the patron of **620** charities and organisations,
433 of which had been held continuously since her accession

If the Queen lives until 10 September 2015, she will
overtake Victoria as the longest reigning British monarch

Fellow citizens

In 2002 the BBC's 'Great Britons' series attracted 1.6 million votes as to who was the greatest Briton ever. The final rankings were as follows (statistics not from the series):

1 WINSTON CHURCHILL (1874–1965)

Took **3** attempts to get into Sandhurst

2 ISAMBARD KINGDOM BRUNEL (1806–59)

Smoked **40** cigars a day

3 PRINCESS DIANA (1961–97)

On the **sixth** anniversary of her death (2003), **4** bouquets of flowers were left outside the gates of Kensington Palace

4 CHARLES DARWIN (1809–82)

The Church of England issued an apology 'for misunderstanding you and, by getting our first reaction wrong, encouraging others to misunderstand you still'. The occasion they chose for this apology was the **200th** anniversary of Darwin's birth

5 WILLIAM SHAKESPEARE (1564–1616)

Wrote only **1** play without a song in it (*The Comedy of Errors*)

6 ISAAC NEWTON (1643–1727)

Served **2** spells as Member of Parliament
for Cambridge University, but made only **1**
speech (to ask if the window might be closed)

7 ELIZABETH I (1533–1603)

Lost all her hair at the age of **29**, because of smallpox, hence the wig.
The disease also left her with scars, hence the white make-up

8 JOHN LENNON (1940–80)

Chose **3** figures for the cover of *Sgt Pepper's Lonely
Hearts Club Band* who were deemed too controversial to
include (Adolf Hitler, Jesus Christ and Mahatma Gandhi)

9 LORD NELSON (1758–1805)

Was **5 foot 4 inches** (1.6 metres) tall

10 OLIVER CROMWELL (1599–1658)

After his body had been exhumed and beheaded, the
head was put on a **25-foot** pole on top of Westminster
Hall, where it stayed for **24** years until it blew off

The capital

URBAN SPRAWL

Today, there are 426 agglomerations in the world with over 1 million people. London is the **19th** largest (with nearly **12 million**), Western Europe's largest. 51 of the 426 are in the USA

There are **126** people per acre in London

In 2007 Tower Hamlets had the lowest working-age employment rate in the UK (**57%**), while the City of London had the highest (**89%**)

THE COSMOPOLITAN CITY

21% of London residents in 2001 were born outside the EU

Over **1 million** Londoners speak a language other than English at home

Top 10 languages (after English) spoken fluently by London schoolchildren:

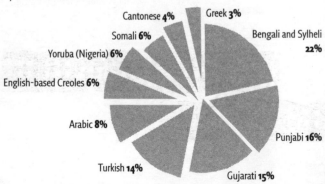

Greek **3%**

Cantonese **4%**

Somali **6%**

Yoruba (Nigeria) **6%**

English-based Creoles **6%**

Arabic **8%**

Turkish **14%**

Bengali and Sylheli **22%**

Punjabi **16%**

Gujarati **15%**

UNDERGROUND

58% of the London Underground is overground

> The shortest distance between any of the **268** Tube stations is between Leicester Square and Covent Garden on the Piccadilly line: **0.16** miles

> The Tube's **412** escalators do the combined equivalent of **2** round-the-world trips every week

OVERGROUND

> London's Routemaster bus was made between 1954 and 1968. They had an anticipated lifespan of **17** years – but were in fact built so strongly that of the **2,876** constructed, approximately **1,000** are still in existence, some of them still running on **2** of the capital's bus routes (**9** and **15**)

> In December 1989, **354** pupils from Churnet View Middle School, Leek, Staffordshire, managed to squeeze in a standard **56**-seater London double-decker bus

The countryside

A Channel 4 survey, based on analysis of such factors as crime levels, education, employment and lifestyle, came up with the 10 best and the 10 worst places to live in the UK. Rural areas featured heavily in the 'best' list:

Best	Ranking	Worst
Epsom and Ewell	1	Hull
City of Westminster	2	Nottingham
Harrogate	3	Strabane
Ashford, Kent	4	Hackney
Stratford-on-Avon	5	Middlesbrough
East Hertfordshire	6	Mansfield
South Cambridgeshire	7	Blaenau Gwent
Mole Valley	8	Merthyr Tydfil
Guildford	9	Salford
West Oxfordshire	10	Easington

A survey by the Commission for Rural Communities in 2007 found that living in the country cost **£60** per week more than in towns and cities

There are **400,000** fewer people aged between **15** and **29** living in rural areas than 20 years ago

Owing to the changing climate there are nearly **400** vineyards in England and Wales

Almost **233,000** people live in an area without a Post Office within **1.25** miles (2 kilometres), or a bank, building society or cash machine within **2.5** miles (4 kilometres)

MOVING AROUND THE COUNTRY

In the 20th century industrial decline
meant that there was an overall movement
of population from the industrial centres of
northern England, Scotland and Wales
to the Midlands and Southeast

This trend has now reversed, with the North
gaining in population every year since 2001
and the South recording a slight decline

There was a net loss
of **83,000** people
from London in 2007

The lie of the land

The UK covers **94,526** square miles (244,821 square kilometres), making it the **79th** largest country in the world

You could fit the UK into Russia **70** times, Australia **31** times, and France **twice**

UK   Russia

On the other hand, the UK could house **8** Belgiums, **345** Singapores and **124,564** Monacos

VITAL STATISTICS

The British Isles is made up of **6,289** islands, of which **803** are large enough to have been digitised with a coastline by Ordnance Survey

With **11,072** miles (17,820 kilometres) of coastline it is the largest island in Europe and the ninth largest in the world (the largest is Greenland). It is the **3rd** most populated island, after Java in Indonesia and Honshu in Japan

The UK's longest river is the Severn: **220** miles (354 kilometres). This is only a twentieth as long as the world's longest rivers – the Nile at **4,135** miles (6,650 kilometres) and the Amazon at **3,980** miles (6,500 kilometres)

Its highest mountain is Ben Nevis: **4,409** feet (1,344 metres), or, put another way, **24,622** feet (7,505 metres) shorter than Everest. It attracts **100,000** ascents per year

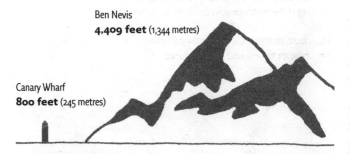

Ben Nevis
4,409 feet (1,344 metres)

Canary Wharf
800 feet (245 metres)

Its largest lake by area is Lough Neagh in Northern Ireland; the largest by volume is Loch Ness in Scotland, which at its deepest is **754** feet (230 metres) – deeper than the height of the BT Tower in London, which is **625** feet (191 metres). It contains more fresh water than all the lakes in England and Wales combined

The furthest point from the sea in the UK is just outside the village of Coton in Derbyshire. From there the nearest section of coast is Fosdyke Wash, on the edge of the Wash, south of Boston in Lincolnshire – **70 miles** (113 kilometres) away

The lowest point is Holme Fen – **9 feet** (2.75 metres) below sea level

One of the after-effects of the last Ice Age is that Britain is slowly tilting, with the southeast sinking and Scotland rising up. The tilt rate is about **0.12** inches (3.10 millimetres) per year – or about the thickness of **8** pages of this book

Flora and fauna

IF YOU GO DOWN TO THE WOODS ...

In 2001 the total area of woodland in Great Britain was **6.7 million** acres (2.7 million hectares) – an increase of over **900,000** acres (360,000 hectares) in the previous decade. That said, only **11.8%** of the land is covered by forest

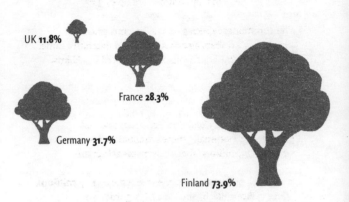

UK **11.8%**

France **28.3%**

Germany **31.7%**

Finland **73.9%**

Within the UK, Scotland is the most densely wooded country (**17%** of land area)

The commonest tree in the UK is the Sitka spruce, followed by the pine, and then – some way behind – the oak and the birch

FEATHERED FRIENDS

The number of farmland birds is **55-60%** of the 1970 value, with some farmland birds (such as the skylark) down to **40%**

Woodland birds are down to **70-5%** of their 1970 numbers. The decline has been blamed on the changing composition of our woodland

Seabirds, by contrast, are up by **32%**

The commonest species seen in gardens since the first survey **40** years ago have remained much the same: they include starlings, house sparrows and blackbirds

FURRY BEASTS

The field vole is reckoned to be the commonest countryside mammal – there are estimated to be some **75 million** (about 1.25 to every human)

The next most numerous are the common shrew (**41.7 million**), wood mouse (**38.0 million**) and rabbit (**37.5 million**)

Grey squirrels outnumber the native red squirrel by **66 to 1**

URBAN DWELLERS

It has been estimated that there are somewhere between **65** and **80** million rats in the UK

Londoners are rarely more than **20 feet** (6 metres) from a rat

There are approximately **33,000** foxes living in urban areas

Insects, flowers and others

INSECTS

Butterflies have been worse affected than plants or other animals by the UK's changing countryside: **5** native species of butterfly have become extinct since the 1970s, and over **three-quarters** of our 59 resident species are declining

The UK has **18** true bumblebee species, the rarest of which (the Great Yellow) is only found in the Highlands and Islands of Scotland

12 species of spider in the UK are known to bite humans. Perhaps not surprisingly, therefore, nearly **50%** of women and **10%** of men have some degree of arachnophobia

The top 3 reasons for disliking spiders:

size

colour of body

length of legs

PLANTS AND FLOWERS

In 2008 both brambles and stinging nettles were in the **top 10** of the UK's most common countryside plants, at numbers **4** and **7** respectively. In 1990 they had been numbers **11** and **14**. The top 3 were rye grass, Yorkshire fog grass and false-oat grass

The top **3** fastest decreasing plants were black bryony, wood avens and ivy, with the wild strawberry in **6th** place and the water forget-me-not in **9th** place

OUT OF THE ORDINARY

Between 2000 and 2006 there were over 10,000 reported sightings of exotic animals in the wild. These included:

- **5,931** big cats (including panthers, pumas, leopards, lynx and jungle cats)
- **3,389** sharks
- **332** wild boars
- **13** dangerous spiders (including a tarantula and a black widow)
- **10** crocodiles
- **7** wolves
- **3** pandas
- **2** scorpions
- **1** penguin

Adders bite over **100** people each year but only **14** resulting deaths have been reported since 1876

The weather

EXTREME WEATHER

 Highest temperature on record: **38.5°C**, Faversham, Kent, 10 August 2003 (the average maximum August temperature from 1971 to 2000 across the UK was 18.9°C)

 Lowest temperature: **-27.2°C**, Braemar, Aberdeenshire, 11 February 1895 and 10 January 1982, and Altnaharra, Highland, 30 December 1995 (the average minimum temperature across the UK from 1971 to 2000 was 1.5°C for December, 0.7°C for January and 0.6°C for February)

 Highest level of monthly sunshine: **383.9 hours**, Eastbourne, Sussex, July 1911 (the average hours of sunshine in July across the UK from 1971 to 2000 was 174.3)

 Highest gust speed (low-level site): **123 knots** (142 miles per hour), Fraserburgh, Aberdeenshire, 13 February 1989

 Highest gust speed (high-level site): **150 knots** (173 miles per hour), summit of Cairngorm, 20 March 1986

 Highest 24-hour rainfall total: **11 inches** (279 millimetres), Martinstown, Dorset, 18 July 1955 (the average rainfall for July across the UK from 1971 to 2000 was 2.7 inches (69.6 millimetres))

 There are up to **40** tornadoes each year in the UK

 The great storm of 24 November to 2 December 1703 killed an estimated **15,000** people; the great storm of 15–16 October 1987 killed **19** people

The floods of 2007 were the worst in the UK for **60** years

The heaviest hailstones recorded weighed **5 ounces** (142 grams) and fell on 5 September 1958 at Horsham, West Sussex (the heaviest hailstones in the world weighed over **2 pounds** each (1 kilogram) and were reported to have killed **92** people in Bangladesh in 1986)

The most lethal fog on record was 'The Great Smog' of London, which lasted from 5 to 9 December 1952. It may have killed anywhere between **4,000** and **12,000** people. Smogs virtually disappeared with the passing of the Clean Air Act of 1956

As recently as the early 1960s, pollution meant that winter sunshine totals were **30%** lower in inner London than in rural areas surrounding the capital. Now the levels are virtually equal

COLD ENOUGH FOR YOU?

The winter of 1947 was one of the coldest on record. From 22 January to 17 March in 1947 snow fell every day somewhere in the UK

The 1962–3 winter was the coldest in England and Wales since 1740. A blizzard on 29–30 December left snowdrifts **20 feet** (6 metres) deep

On 2 February 2009, **11 inches** (30 centimetres) of snow resulted in 20% of Britain's workforce enjoying a 'snow day'. So badly were the roads affected that all London buses were cancelled for the day – something that hadn't happened during the Blitz or in the winters of 1947 and 1963. Industry experts estimated the snow day's cost to the economy to be **£1 billion**

Green Britain?

The nation produces enough solid waste
to fill the Albert Hall every hour

85% of waste ends up in landfill. Figures from
2004–5 show that the UK sends the same amount
of rubbish to landfill as the **18** EU countries with
lowest landfill rates combined, even though those
countries have almost twice our population

The average Briton produces **10** carbon tonnes each year

At 2007's Live Earth concert at Wembley,
5 of the top acts together had an annual
output of almost **2,000** carbon tonnes.
Madonna alone had an annual carbon
footprint of **1,018** tonnes

Redland, in Bristol, has the highest proportion of residents worried
about the environment and trying to do something about it. More
than **8 out of 10** adults in Redland are classified as 'enthusiastic
greens' – over **5** times the national average.

The least green area is the centre of Basildon, Essex,
where over **4 out of 10** are 'environmentally unconcerned'

5% of electricity generated in the UK in
2007 came from renewable resources

WORST-CASE SCENARIOS

If current warming trends continue unabated,
it is predicted that by the 2080s:

- the south of England will feel as warm at midnight
  on summer evenings as it does at 7pm today

- sea levels will be **70** centimetres higher at the southern end
  of the UK, and **50** centimetres higher along the northwestern
  coast. **2 million** extra people will be at risk of flooding

- French grape varieties could be harvested
  on the slopes of the Lake District

ETERNAL OPTIMISM

2007 public opinion survey conducted by the Department
for the Environment, Food and Rural Affairs:

'Humans are capable of finding ways to overcome
the world's environmental problems'
Tend to agree/strongly agree: **67%**

'Scientists will find a solution to global warming without
people having to make big changes to their lifestyles'
Tend to agree/strongly agree: **19%**

'Climate change is beyond control –
it's too late to do anything about it'
Tend to agree/strongly agree: **17%**

The next generation

Each year since 2005 Luton First has conducted a survey of 10-year-olds. Here's a selection of their findings:

What do you think is the very best thing in the world?

2008	2005
Good looks	Being rich
Being rich	Being famous
Being famous	Football
Being happy	Pop music
The internet	Animals

What do you think is the very worst thing in the world?

2008	2005
Being fat	Drunk people
Divorce	Smoking
Drunk people	Litter
Being poor	Graffiti
Terrorists	War

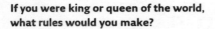

If you were king or queen of the world, what rules would you make?

2008	2005
No divorces	No telling lies
No bullying	No getting drunk
No knives and guns	No fighting and killing
No getting drunk	No drugs
No cancer	No knives and guns

Who is the most famous person in all the world?

2008 | *2005*

2008	2005
Simon Cowell	God
God	Wayne Rooney
The Queen	Jesus
Father Christmas	David Beckham
Harry Potter	The Queen

Do you think you will get married when you grow up?

2008

Yes: **81%**

2005

Yes: **72%**

66% of children surveyed said they were happy

AND FINALLY ...

1 in 100 of those born in 1900 reached the age of **100**

Nearly **1 in 4** of those born in 2001 will reach the age of **100**

References

While researching this book I have consulted a whole range of different sources (many of which contradict each other!). By far the most important is the Office of National Statistics (ONS) (www.statistics.gov.uk) which covers practically every aspect of life in Britain. Its Social Trends reports are particularly fascinating and useful. I have also looked at reports issued by various government departments, notably the Department of Health, Department of Transport, Department for Business (formerly Trade and Industry), the Home Office and the Ministry of Defence. The national census, carried out every 10 years, is a great source of information about topics such as population, ethnicity and religious beliefs. The House of Commons has issued various reports and research papers that are useful for facts about Parliament and economic and social trends. Other good sources include the various British Crime Surveys, the Met Office website and the websites for the agencies that are responsible for the countryside, including the Forestry Commision. The BBC website has been invaluable, as has Eurostat for European statistics, and the CIA handbook and UN for international ones.

It would be impossible to list references for every fact in the book – many have been derived from a whole range and combination of sources, both official and unofficial. Below, however, I have listed some specific surveys and sources (non-official or government) that have proved particularly helpful.

People Top 20 first names: 2008 Bounty survey. Teenage pregnancy figures: *Daily Express* (14/2/2002). Marriage surveys: Norwich Union (6/08), Condé Nast (8/6/09) and GMC Discos (28/9/2008). Divorce figures: Grant Thornton survey (2/2008), the United Nations Economic Commission for Europe. Celebrity divorce settlement figures: *Guardian* (4/8/2006), *Daily Telegraph* (21/11/2008), *The Times* (24/10/2005), *Daily Telegraph* (17/8/2008). Main causes of death: BBC (25/5/06). Suicide rates after Princess Diana's death: *British Medical Journal* (18/11/2000). Cremation and burial figures: Oddfellows survey (2000).
Where we live Houses and flats: Bradford and Bingley report (2/5/2002). The small size of British homes: *Independent* (11/2/2009). House prices: BBC (7/11/2008) and *Marketing* magazine (14/10/2008). Expensive homes: *Daily Express* (22/10/2007) and *The Times* (15/3/2007). Updown Court: *Square* magazine (1/5/2007). Cheaper areas of the country: BBC (23/4/2007). Kitchen statistics: *Plenty and Want*, John Burnet (1989) and Rachel's Organic survey (2007). Bathroom timings: Vaseline survey reported by PR Newswire (24/8/2003) and Milton survey, reported in femalefirst (30/11/2007). MPs' toilet habits: *Independent* (28/10/2001). Toilet habits of the wider population: 2008 Tearfund survey for World Toilet Day (19/11/2008) and a Cancer Research Fund survey, reported in the *Guardian*

(29/3/2001). Sleeping habits: the Sleep Council for National Bed Month (3/2008). Value of children's possessions: Lloyds TSB Insurance survey, reported by the BBC (1/2/2006). Sleeping positions: Travelodge survey, reported by the BBC (7/10/2006). Snoring: www.britishsnoring.co.uk. Dreams: Shattered National Sleep survey, reported by Channel 4 (10/1/2009). Ford Focus: *Auto Trader* (15/2/2008). Driving test: *Guardian* (3/9/2008). Car love-making: Diamond survey (2/2008). **The working week** Time-wasting at work: salary.com (27/8/2008). Office romance and porn: *Daily Telegraph* (29/1/2009). Average salaries: BBC 2008 study. Dangerous jobs: Risk Placement Services report (7/2007) and Oxford University research, reported by the BBC (16/8/2002). Morality in the workplace: surveys by Mintel, Powerchex and the Risk Advisory Group. Absence from work: CBI survey, reported by the BBC (10/4/2007). Work Foundation survey: reported on personneltoday.com (19/7/2006). **Our obsessions** Walking: Rambler's Association website. Leisure activities of retired people: *Daily Telegraph* (3/2/2007). Knitting figures: UK Handknitting Association website. Top 5 TV audiences: British Film Institute. Which channels we watch: ITC viewing figures and the *Daily Telegraph* (10/4/2007). Top 10 celebrity role models: *Sun* (14/3/2008). Top 10 'love to hate' figures: onepoll.com (2008). Atom bombs vs Reality TV: BBC survey (21/5/2008). Time spent on-line: *The Times Online* (2008). Membership of organisations, on-line and off: YouGov poll, reported in the *Guardian* (7/11/2006). The ways in which people make phone calls: Post Office research, reported on www.cellular-news.com (27/3/2006). Impact of the recession on 118118: *Guardian* (17/11/2008). Text messages sent each month: Reuters (11/2008). DIY insurance claims and regional expertise: Woolwich Insurance Services survey (2000). Gardening problems: comparethemarket.com (9/2008). Top 10 'garden gripes': BBC *Gardeners' World* magazine (6/2004). Pets: Pet Food Manufacturers' Association (2009). Drivers and pets: Mori poll (2001). Gambling: Gambling Commission report (National Centre for Social Research) (2007). Behaviour on the *Titanic*: David Savage, Queensland University of Technology, reported by the BBC (21/1/09). Future Foundation survey: reported by the BBC (7/6/2002). Rudeness: *Sunday Times* (21/5/2000). Britons not welcome abroad: Expedia.com survey, reported in the *Daily Telegraph* (19/7/2002). Road rage: Max Power study, reported by the BBC (13/8/2003). **Sport** Food and drink served at Wimbledon: Wimbledon website. Darts: Blue Square survey, reported in the *Daily Telegraph* (9/3/2007). **Our leisure time** London cinema figures: Think London (11/2007). UK cinema admissions: BFI. Recalling adverts: Cinema Advertising Association, reported in *Brand Republic* (5/2/2008). Sleeping habits in cinemas: Orange film survey, reported by the BBC (29/1/2001). Theatregoers: Whatsonstage. com, reported by the BBC (13/7/2001). Most-played songs in public places: BBC Radio 2 poll (13/4/2009). Expenditure on holidays: BBC (21/1/2007). Thefts from hotels: Hotels.com survey (2005). **Getting around** Relaxation on holiday: American Express survey (2008). UK motorways: RAC (2006). Slow-moving traffic: keepmoving.co.uk, reported in the *Daily Mail* (17/1/2008). Sat Navs: DirectLine survey for the *Daily Mirror* (22/7/2008). Overcrowding on trains: *Daily Telegraph* (15/10/2008). Laptops lost at Heathrow: Dell survey (July 2008). Manchester airport: BBC (26/11/2003). **Fashion** Women finding buying clothes depressing: www.ksl.com (18/8/2008). Time spent on buying clothes: Fish4homes, reported by the BBC (23/6/2002). Best and worst fashion items: www.missbutterfly.com, reported in the *Lancashire Evening Telegraph* (18/7/2007). Managers' attitudes to make-up: *The Times* (29/11/2007). Women's dress sizes: *Health of Britain – Perspectives on Nutrition 2008*, www.trisglobal.com; *Daily Telegraph* (8/4/09). How many items and how long women keep them for: Clothes Show Live survey, reported in the *Daily Telegraph* (4/12/2008). How many pairs of shoes do you own: *Daily Mail* (9/8/2006). Men and ties: *Guardian* (5/9/2006). Underwear: Marks & Spencer survey. What Scotsmen wear under their kilts: Famous Grouse survey. **Food and drink** Yoghurts: BBC (9/5/2008). Yoghurts wasted: Waste and Resources Action Programme, reported by the BBC (9/5/2009). Luxury food: know your money blog (26/8/2008). Perfect meals: *Plenty and Want*, John Burnet (1989). Curry: *Tandori* magazine mediapack. Chicken tikka masala: *Real Curry Restaurant Guide* (1998). Fish and chips: *Daily Telegraph* (17/8/2008). Restaurants: Horizons/Foodservice Intelligence. Tipping: *Which?* (25/9/2008). Restaurant etiquette: Ashburton Cookery School survey (2006). Unhealthy snacking: *Sun* (7/5/2008), Aldi survey (6/5/2009). Chocolate consumption: FlyerTalk forum (2003). Tea: United Kingdom Tea Council, ActionAid survey (18/2/2008). Bottled water: www.britishbottledwater.org. Rise of wine: Mintel, www.aim-digest.com. Decline of pubs: British Beer and Pub Association (16/10/2006). **The nation's health** Fat Britain: National Obesity Forum research, reported in the *Daily Telegraph* (11/11/2008). Women's concern about their figures: *Top Santé* survey, reported in the *Guardian* (12/10/2000). Teeth: Genix Healthcare survey, reported in the *Guardian* (1/5/2008). Dentists' income coming from private work: Laing & Buisson survey, reported by the BBC (6/1/2005). Cost of fillings: *Daily Mail* (10/1/2008). Eyesight: Association of Contact Lens Manufactuers and RNIB. Pride in the NHS: BBC (30/6/2008). Cosmetic surgery: British Association of Aesthetic Plastic Surgeons (2008). Plastic surgery as a gift: *Which?* (12/2008). Smoking: BBC (29/6/2007). Drugs: *Daily Telegraph* (19/4/2007). **The nation's wealth** Farming: *Farmer's Guardian* (17/4/2009). Motoring costs: RAC survey, reported on the BBC (9/7/2008). Rise of the supermarket: University of Exeter research. Cash machines: APACS (2006). Broke Britain: Credit Action (4/2009). The Rich: *The Sunday Times Rich List* (2009). Jobs and private education: Sutton Trust (2007). Best-selling books: Nielsen BookScan. Unreadable books: Teletext poll (2007). Everyday words: British National Corpus. Swearing: *Daily Telegraph* (16/1/2009). Dumb Britain: *Daily Mail* (19/3/2009, looking at various surveys, including those by the Dairy Farmers of Britain, and Walt Disney Studios Home Entertainment in conjunction with the Royal Astonomical Society); *Times Higher Education* magazine (7/8/2008). Relative IQs: *IQs and the Wealth of Nations*, Lynn and Vanhanen (2002). **Politics** Working class and middle class: Liverpool Victorian Friendly Society survey, reported by the BBC (5/5/2006); *Middle Britain*, William Nelson, reported in *The Times* (5/5/2006). Upper class: *Independent* (2/2/2005). **Religion** Belief in the Devil: *Independent* (25/3/2007). The fundamental question: Mori poll for BBC Horizon (1/2006). Belief in aliens: *Focus* magazine, reported by the BBC (13/1/1999). Age and beliefs: Mori poll (2005). **Crime and punishment** CCTV: Crimestoppers, reported by the BBC (26/3/2007). Police officers with criminal records: *Guardian* (11/3/2009). **War and Peace** Military powers: Wikipedia (2008). Nuclear club: BBC (21/4/2009). **The great and the good** Great Britons: BBC (2002). **Town and country** Languages spoken in London: National Centre for Languages. Town vs country: Channel 4 survey (2005). **Green and pleasant land** Exotic animals in the wild: BeastwatchUK, reported in the *Daily Mail* (18/9/2006). **The next generation** 10-year-old findings: Lutonfirst.com.